The College Roommate

FROM HELL

Skills and Strategies for Surviving College With a Problem Roommate

By Linda Fiore

THE COLLEGE ROOMMATE FROM HELL: SKILLS AND STRATEGIES FOR SURVIVING COLLEGE WITH A PROBLEM ROOMMATE

Copyright © 2009 by Atlantic Publishing Group, Inc.
1405 SW 6th Ave. • Ocala, Florida 34471 • 800-814-1132 • 352-622-1875–Fax
Web site: www.atlantic-pub.com • E-mail: sales@atlantic-pub.com
SAN Number: 268-1250

ISBN-13: 978-1-60138-276-4   ISBN-10: 1-60138-276-6

Library of Congress Cataloging-in-Publication Data

Fiore, Linda, 1956-
  The college roommate from hell : skills and strategies for surviving college with a problem roommate / by Linda Fiore.
     p. cm.
  Includes bibliographical references and index.
  ISBN-13: 978-1-60138-276-4 (alk. paper)
  ISBN-10: 1-60138-276-6 (alk. paper)
  1. College students--Social conditions. 2. Roommates. 3. College student orientation. 4. Interpersonal relations. I. Title.
  LB3607.F56 2008
  646.70088'378198--dc22
                              2008035552

INTERIOR LAYOUT DESIGN: Nicole Deck • ndeck@atlantic-pub.com
PROJECT MANAGER: Melissa Peterson • mpeterson@atlantic-pub.com

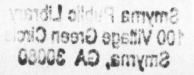

We recently lost our beloved pet "Bear," who was not only our best and dearest friend but also the "Vice President of Sunshine" here at Atlantic Publishing. He did not receive a salary but worked tirelessly 24 hours a day to please his parents. Bear was a rescue dog that turned around and showered myself, my wife Sherri, his grandparents Jean, Bob and Nancy and every person and animal he met (maybe not rabbits) with friendship and love. He made a lot of people smile every day.

We wanted you to know that a portion of the profits of this book will be donated to The Humane Society of the United States.

–Douglas & Sherri Brown

THE HUMANE SOCIETY
OF THE UNITED STATES ©

The human-animal bond is as old as human history. We cherish our animal companions for their unconditional affection and acceptance. We feel a thrill when we glimpse wild creatures in their natural habitat or in our own backyard.

Unfortunately, the human-animal bond has at times been weakened. Humans have exploited some animal species to the point of extinction.

The Humane Society of the United States makes a difference in the lives of animals here at home and worldwide. The HSUS is dedicated to creating a world where our relationship with animals is guided by compassion. We seek a truly humane society in which animals are respected for their intrinsic value, and where the human-animal bond is strong.

Want to help animals? We have plenty of suggestions. Adopt a pet from a local shelter, join The Humane Society and be a part of our work to help companion animals and wildlife. You will be funding our educational, legislative, investigative and outreach projects in the U.S. and across the globe.

Or perhaps you'd like to make a memorial donation in honor of a pet, friend or relative? You can through our Kindred Spirits program. And if you'd like to contribute in a more structured way, our Planned Giving Office has suggestions about estate planning, annuities, and even gifts of stock that avoid capital gains taxes.

Maybe you have land that you would like to preserve as a lasting habitat for wildlife. Our Wildlife Land Trust can help you. Perhaps the land you want to share is a backyard—that's enough. Our Urban Wildlife Sanctuary Program will show you how to create a habitat for your wild neighbors.

So you see, it's easy to help animals. And The HSUS is here to help.

The Humane Society of the United States
2100 L Street NW
Washington, DC 20037
202-452-1100
www.hsus.org

Dedication

This book is dedicated to Isabelle Lian.

Table of Contents

Chapter 2: Once You Are There   61

Chapter 5: Cultural and Social Differences

Chapter 6: When There Is A Serious Problem

129

147

Chapter 7: Conflict, Cooperation, and Compromise 179

Foreword

Megan O'Leary-Buda

Congratulations, you have been accepted to college! Get ready, your life is about to change. Deciding to live on-campus is an even more exciting, though sometimes challenging, experience. College life is completely different than anything a young adult faces in high school. The best preparation is to know exactly what to expect. Although you cannot plan for every milestone, you can start college prepared with knowledge from others who have been there before. Determining how to be prepared for a successful life in college requires you to look at the issues from the perspectives of many different people.

Living the college life is more than just hanging around in a dorm room with friends like you see in the movies. There is more to life in a residence hall than just cork boards and concert posters. You will have much more to deal with than trying to decide which party to attend while still attempting to wake up for that 8:00 a.m. sociology class. Add in a new person to live with, whom you have never met, and your life will again take a new spin.

Frequently, a new college roommate can cause you to view your life and the world differently. Sharing items may be a new concept and dealing with someone's quirks may try your last nerve. While a troublesome roommate can be a challenge, Linda Fiore, author of *The College Roommate from Hell: Skills and Strategies for Surviving College With a Problem Roommate*, provides a complete guide for college life. She arms you with the essential college student handbook, providing details on what to expect in the months before you attend your first semester to dealing with those crazy habits a new roommate will bring into your life.

Since it wasn't long ago that I was a college student, I can attest that this book is exactly what I could have used to help my friends with their troublesome roommates. In my current position as a residence hall director, I work to help students transition into college and assist in their personal development on a daily basis. Specifically, each semester my position requires me to answer questions from students and parents. The suggestions that I give on roommate and mediation issues are not just for first year students, but upperclassmen as well. This book offers the same advice that I often give to my new students and I am sure that it will be a resource that you will refer back to often as issues arise with your new roommate.

Frequently, students are very excited about going to college, but do not prepare in a way that will truly help them. College preparation is more than just scheduling your classes so that you will be able to graduate on time. Living on a college campus is an intricate new world. Learning more about yourself before you arrive will assist you in determining your compatibility with a new roommate.

In the book, Fiore lays out a clear path for success so that new students can begin on the right track and have a rewarding college experience. The setup of the book is extremely reader friendly. After each chapter, she even offers helpful words of wisdom that sum up the topic at hand. This is a great summary for understanding the real life of a college student.

While it's expected that life at college will eventually throw some curves in your plan, the information in this book is intended to assist you in making conscious decisions about how you can change your life. Even if your idea of the perfect college roommate does not pan out, this book will assist you in finding new ways to deal with that different, and sometimes difficult, roommate. Remember that there is more to a college roommate than just their schedule and their musical interests. Ultimately, their lifestyle may have an impact on your life, too. The best advice is to come to college prepared for the worst, but hoping for the best. The more intricate details of a person's life will appear as you begin to live together. You may come to think of your roommate as a best friend or you may avoid them at all costs. You may even become a guiding force in your roommate's life.

A student's transition into college may be difficult to understand. Even if you are able to acclimate yourself well to new atmospheres, reading this book may help you assist others in their self-discovery. Fiore offers real life stories from college students about many situations that you will face yourself, such as having difficult conversations about sexuality, mediating conflicts, eating disorders, and many more. Frequently students can come prepared with the right sized sheets, but have no idea how to help others with these larger issues that come along with living in a residence hall. Keeping an open mind about other lifestyles and personal interests will only enhance your ability to live with people who are different than you.

Most of this book will show you how to handle the situations on your own. However, sometimes you can only do so much. While rooming with a new person may not always work out, Fiore also offers guidance in mediation and working with residential life professionals. Students and parents alike can gain much needed advice from Fiore. Take all of her tips into consideration while preparing for college life. Remember, no one has a right way, but *The College Roommate from Hell: Skills and Strategies for Surviving College With a Problem Roommate* offers expert advice from administrators and students who have lived through it. I wish you luck with your new transition to the awesome world of college.

Megan O'Leary-Bud
Residence Hall Director, Off Campus Properties
Quinnipiac University

Megan O'Leary-Buda holds a Bachelor of Arts in History and Religion from Ashland University. While there, she worked with students and assisted in their transition into campus life as a Resident Assistant. During the completion of her master's degree in higher education administration at The University of Akron, she developed assessment tools and strategic planning for the Department of Student Life. She has written many articles for **www.collegeview.com** *and* **www. gradview.com** *regarding college life including:*

- *What to Expect When You Arrive at College: Getting acquainted with your surroundings and adjusting to college life*

- *Sharing a Room: Preparing to share your space and your stuff for the first time*

- *College Dorm Life: Sharing your space, shower, laundry facility, and more*

- *Meeting New People: Finding friends you'll have forever*

- *The Scholarship Application Process*

- *What to Bring to College: Helping you pack for your first year*

- *Q&A with a Financial Aid Office*

Megan currently works for Quinnipiac University as a residence hall director for off-campus properties. There, she is able to work with true transfer students in an apartment community, as well as sophomore and junior students living in university owned neighborhoods. Additionally, she supervises resident assistants for these areas who provide support for those residential students.

Introduction

I attended a small music conservatory in New England, and the "dorm" rooms were situated in nothing that resembled a dormitory. Instead, our "dorm" was in the dark basement of one of the buildings, sandwiched between piano-practice rooms. My two roommates and I claimed our own corners of the room and set up beds, desks, chairs, and bureaus. We jointly decorated the room with lava lamps, macramé wall hangings, and posters depicting the images of Bach, Leonard Bernstein, and Jesus on the cross. What can I say? It was the '70s and we were music geeks.

One of my roommates was a New-York born, musical theater major who offered selections from "Carousel" and "The Music Man" without provocation. The word "actress" could not have suited her better, as numerous "leading men" visited her to "read scripts" through the night and into the next morning. My other roommate was a buttoned-up, born-again Christian opera major from an elite town outside Boston. She arose every morning at 5 a.m. to lead her prayer group in the practice room across the hall. I fell somewhere in between: a homesick piano major who just wanted to do well in school and get along with everyone.

Even though our backgrounds, life styles, and majors were different, we managed to get along in our big, wall-free room;

respect each other's needs; stay out of each other's way; and make fun of each other in a friendly way. We also stayed in touch post-college and have tracked each other's careers.

Did we have much in common? Not really. But we had found common ground in our love for music and our dream to turn that passion into successful careers. Let's face it: no one attends a music conservatory to study landscape design. We also had no money, and as music majors, which required hours of practice and rehearsals each week in addition to a full class load, no time left for a job. We'd scrape up our quarters and walk over to Fenway Pizza for a slice, or pay student admission to see the Red Sox and sit on the steps, which you could do back in those days. In sum, we were quite different but enjoyed each other's company and had a lot of fun.

Even though much is different for college students in 2008, some of the same challenges of living with total strangers in a cramped space are as true today as they were 30 years ago. College roommates not only bring luggage to their hall on move-in day; they can bring emotional and life-style baggage as well. This book will help prepare incoming freshmen for life in a dorm, with plenty of tips on cohabitating with and surviving life with the problem roommate.

Notes to the Reader

Throughout this book you will become friends with "KIM." No, KIM is not the organized, smart, witty roommate who lets you use her shampoo and shares the homemade cookies Mom sent from Ohio, but rather a series of reminders or brief summaries of important things to "Keep In Mind:" K-I-M.

1. When referring to a roommate, "him," "her," "she," and "he" are used interchangeably without preference given to either gender.

2. "Residence hall" refers to an on-campus, student-designated building. The terms "residence hall," "hall," and "dorm" are used interchangeably.

3. "Housing office" also refers to "office of residential life," or "office of residence life."

4. "RD" refers to resident director, a person who oversees other staff within the residence hall. At some universities that person may be the resident assistant, or "RA." For purposes of consistency, throughout this book "RD" refers to the staff member with highest level of authority within the residence hall or dorm and to whom other members report.

1

What to Expect

Before You Arrive

You have filled out the housing questionnaire and roommate preference forms. You may have embellished a bit along the way. Maybe you tend to kick stale pizza crusts under your bed on occasion but selected the "I prefer a neat roommate" check box. Perhaps you like to study from midnight to 3 a.m., but noted you are an "early riser." Campus housing professionals will tell you the first rule in submitting roommate preferences is to be honest. The first rule is to send your deposit and application in on time, but we will assume you are now a responsible adult and this does not apply to you.

If you are allergic to cigarette smoke, do not indicate that you do not mind living with a smoker, because the consequences will result in resentment and possibly some health issues. If you tend to be on the shy side and it takes a while before you open up, do not paint yourself as someone who is outgoing. It is that simple. Portraying yourself as someone you are not is not going to make you a more attractive roommate or popular student. You will be confronted with a difficult situation if you get matched with a loud, obnoxious party animal who was honest with her preferences. This process is similar to online dating. You can create a fictional "you" to appear more likeable, but the time will come when you have to meet the other person face-to-face.

This is also not the time to experiment with reverse psychology. Indicating that you are a neat freak in your preferences when you are not, does not mean you will get assigned to a neat freak who will do all the cleaning. Also, do not assume that if you are matched with an honors student, that person will help you study. The exact opposite will happen. This person will resent your laziness, lack of enthusiasm, and dirty dishes in the sink, and will wonder how in the world she ended up rooming with a slob like yours truly.

Moving into a hall, and even starting college, is a huge step to adulthood. It can be overwhelming, especially if you have never lived away from home. If your inclination is to run back to Mom and Dad after the second day, especially if the first impression of your roommate is less than stellar, give it at least a few weeks. Just like your first day of kindergarten, everything gets easier with time. You will meet new people from all kinds of backgrounds right away. You would have to go out of your way not to meet new people. They are everywhere: down the hall, in the cafeteria, sitting next to you in class, and at social gatherings. You are not the only person who may not know anyone else on campus.

Take a deep breath. Introduce yourself to your roommates. Have a conversation, get to know each other, and then be prepared for them to get on your last nerve and for them to tell you the same. It is just like living with your family, but with different rules and unlimited Internet access.

Welcome to the world of college roommates. Let us hope you do not get assigned to the "one from hell."

KIM: You will, at some point in your career as a hall resident, either be matched with a problem roommate or have a conflict with your roommate. Be prepared to accept conflict as a means to develop problem-solving skills. Also be prepared to enter into this relationship with realistic expectations.

College Roommate, Meet College Roommate

Living with a college roommate can be a rewarding and enriching experience. You will not only learn more about yourself but how to effectively relate to your peers, resolve conflicts, adjust to new situations, and build communication and social skills. For your roommate experience to be a success rather than a failure, you will have to be willing to cooperate and compromise, which will not always be easy. Sharing a room with someone is like a relationship or marriage. There have to be compromise and flexibility for it to work. You will have to accept another person and all her faults. However, when it is over after four years, you can wish each other well, go your own way, and not have to worry about spousal or child-support payments.

Part of the excitement of living on your own and going away to college is experiencing new challenges, meeting new people, and flourishing as an adult. While living independently for the first time can seem daunting, you will be doing so in a safe, supportive environment with peers who are facing the same doubts as you are. In addition to new educational experiences, the experience of sharing a small space with other students is an education in itself. Your roommate may come from a different cultural, religious, or economic background. He may have grown up on a farm in Iowa, whereas you may have lived in a New York high-rise. She may be Jewish; you may be a devout Catholic. His family may be involved in every major decision he makes, while yours is letting you find your way.

Residence halls are communities. As you will read later on, some are structured communities based on shared interests and academic areas. There are students who take full advantage of what the halls have to offer. Opportunities to socialize and participate in activities are plentiful, including concerts, movies, theme-nights, workshops, and seminars on topics ranging from stress management to identity theft. Then there is a different population of students who see their living arrangement on campus as a place to sleep and study because they may have a full social life outside college or may be taking a full load of classes and holding down a job.

A mutual understanding is key to a successful relationship with your roommate, even though it is likely that you will both have different ideas of what the living arrangement will be like and you will have varied expectations. These feelings are normal and shared by almost every college student I spoke to over the course of researching this book. Remember, you are sharing the new college and new-roommate experience with thousands of other 18-year-olds around the country and the world.

Do not let the following pages and horror stories frighten you. During the time I spent talking to dorm residents, either in person, on the phone, or via e-mail, almost all of them had good things to say about having a roommate. The consensus is that you have to learn to live with each other's faults and annoyances, but it is part of growing up and living independently. Granted, you may encounter the "crazy" roommate, the roommate who spent four years getting drunk every weekend, or the roommate who considered wandering the dorm halls naked normal behavior.

Life as a College Roommate

Before people go into surgery, it seems as though everyone they encounter, has a story to tell about what either went wrong with them, someone they know or about something they read. These stories can fall under the heading, "Surgery Stories from Hell." It is the same when a woman is expecting a baby. Everyone is an expert on childbirth and child rearing. Some people seem to delight in telling the poor woman all of the horrors that lie ahead when it comes to giving birth and the parenting process. In these instances, people mean well and their intention is not to worry you, but they are trying to better prepare you for a new experience.

To prepare you for the chapters and stories that follow, here are some comments, both good and bad, about life as a college roommate:

- "Your roommate is the first person you'll get to know at college, so you want to make a good impression."

- "After the lights went out, we'd lie in bed and just talk about stuff that was going on in our lives. I'm an only child, so I never had that experience with a sibling."

- "My roommate was a psycho."

- "My roommate spoke little English and I could never figure out why she was even there, but she taught me about her culture and we helped each other understand our roots."

- "We had separate lives but got along great. I think that's the key to a good roommate relationship. Don't hang onto each other too much."

- "If something smells in your room, check under your roommate's bed."

- "My roommate had a definite eating disorder. She would buy two pints of ice cream, eat them both in one sitting, and then go down the hall to the bathroom and throw up. I tried to help, but she was in denial. In my sophomore year, I requested a transfer. I just felt sorry for her."

- "My roommate said she believed in abstinence before

marriage when I first talked to her, but she's had every guy on campus in our room."

- "I lived in a mixed-year dorm and was intimidated by older students at first, but learned a lot from them about school, campus, and life."

- "I never thought this would be part of the picture, but I learned more about myself living with another person than I did in English class. Sharing a cramped space for four years brings out the worst in everyone and I was no exception."

- "I was expecting to have lots of romantic relationships during college but ended up having more roommates than girlfriends. Unfortunately, they were all men."

- "I roomed with a schizo, a bulimic, and a vegan, so I decided not to go in the mental-health field and I have them to thank."

- "It sounds corny, but my roommate became my best friend, and, ten years later, we talk all the time and vacation with each other's families. She did get on my nerves though, and I am sure I did (get on her's) too."

- "If you can get a single somehow, do it. That is my advice. Otherwise, you will be dealing with sex, drugs, and rock 'n' roll all the time, which for some students, may be a good thing. For me, it was a nightmare."

- "My roommate stories were so horrific, a newspaper in Boston featured me in a story it wrote on the subject. Thank goodness I was anonymous."

- "My roommate seemed to think college was nothing

more than a giant keg, and I went to an expensive university. I felt so bad for his parents. They thought he was a golden child and never did anything wrong. Little did they know he drank himself into a stupor every weekend. He didn't even make it through the first semester."

- "I really hit the jackpot. My roommate and I do everything together. I get along with her better than my own sister."

- "If you hear puking from the bathroom and find boxes of doughnuts in the closet, your roommate has an eating disorder."

- "I lived in a suite with five other roommates. I was so glad there weren't just two of us because this way, if someone is in a bad mood, you have four other moods to choose from."

- "My roommate in junior year was from another country and didn't seem to believe in showering. She smelled bad and tried to cover it up with perfume. I couldn't stand to be in the room with her, so I spent that semester living with a friend and then told the housing office one of us had to go. She went."

- "I just finished law school and would live my undergraduate years all over again if I could. I had a blast living in the dorms. I made a ton of friends and our RA planned all these fun events for us. Those were the days."

- "I wear contact lenses and cigarette smoke really

bothers me. I put that on my housing preference form and was matched with someone who wrote the same. No sooner had we introduced ourselves the first day when she sneaked out for a cigarette."

- "I made the mistake of living with a childhood friend our first semester. We ended up fighting constantly over stupid stuff, but it was enough to eventually switch dorms. A whole semester passed when we didn't talk, but then we realized how much our friendship meant to us. We just can't live together."

Rather than paint a rosy pictures of idyllic campus living and dorm sharing, this book presents realistic scenarios you are likely to encounter at some point during your tenure with a college roommate. Unless the conflicts are serious and irresolvable, which some will be, try to be optimistic about this new phase of your life. There is a good chance you will make a new, lifelong friend. There is an even better chance you will learn more about people, life styles, and cultures than you ever did during your previous 18 years.

As in life and your post-college career, look for positive qualities if you find yourself living with someone with opposite tastes and life-style choices. Everyone has interesting qualities, and you may have more in common than you think once you get to know each other. Do not assume the behavior you deem as annoying in your roommate is something he is doing on purpose. If the TV is on all the time, that may have been a study habit he developed years ago, and it most likely never occurred to him that it bothers someone else. Also, no one is a mind reader. If you do not communicate what is troubling you about your roommate, it is not only unfair to him but it does nothing to bring resolution about any faster.

Last, it is four (or maybe five) years of your life and it goes by quickly. Take advantage of everything college has to offer. As life becomes more difficult post-college, you may look back on your roommate experience with fond memories.

> **KIM:** If you have not been truthful about your likes, dislikes, life-style preferences, and other indicators on the roommate preference form, do not be surprised when the person you meet on move-in day is nothing like the kind of person you requested.

Roommate Conflict: An Introduction

To get off on a good foot with your roommate, be open, honest, assertive, in a good way, and respectful of him or her wanting the same. If you are both on the same page as to what the expectations are, how they can be met, and how to monitor them over the next few years to avoid conflict, you will have a good foundation. It is not quite that easy. You will both be coming from different perspectives and will have different visions of what dorm life is like.

Here is what I call a "tip sheet" that summarizes some of the main topics in this book, all of which will be covered in detail. You will want to copy this page and keep it somewhere safe just in case you find yourself not speaking to each other by your sophomore year.

Tip #1 – Every Little Thing She Does is Not Magic

What started out as a minor annoyance you did not think bothered you has, two months later, turned into fingernails on the blackboard and the bane of your existence. Gum chewing, hair twirling, snoring, constant sighing, you name it, and it will eventually get on your nerves. Unless you are in a six-person suite and can actually move around from room to room, you are stuck in the same space with this person, and it is a small one at that. Did your mom ever tell you that patience is a virtue? You may not care if it is a virtue or not, but it is an attitude you will need to develop to accept your roommate and all of his or her faults. Keep in mind you will have yours as well.

Tip #2 – You Mean it is not Just About Me?

In addition to being patient, you will have to be tolerant and considerate of another person. It sounds like a lot to ask, but you would want the same from him or her. Leaving your clothes on the floor, putting an empty milk carton back in the fridge, and blasting YouTube from your PC while your roommate is sleeping does not make for a peaceful environment.

Tip #3 – When is a Guest Not a Guest?

You may think you "own" one-half of the room and can have anyone you want over any time of day as long as he or she stays in your one-half of the room. It does not quite work that way. Be considerate of your roommate's privacy, especially if you plan to do more than study with your guest. Ask first before inviting anyone to stay over.

If you work out an agreement to do so once a week, your roommate should have the same option.

Tip #4 – Living Together Means Never Having to Say. . .

You will, at some point, argue with your roommate, just as you argue with your family, loved ones, and some day, a partner or spouse. Do not hold a grudge for more than a day. Talk it out — do not think you can resolve conflict by text messaging and smiley faces. A conflict may seem overwhelming when it happens, especially when hurt feelings are involved, but in a few years, you may not even remember your roommate's name. Do not assume moving to another dorm will solve your problems. There could be a worse roommate looming right around the corner.

Tip #5 – All is Fair, or so I am Told

Do not wait for each other to clean your room. Unless the cleaning fairy pops in on weekends, you both have to share the responsibility so get over your opposition to operating a vacuum or working a mop and get moving. If a cleaning schedule will work and keep you both on track, switch off responsibilities week to week. If you absolutely cannot live without dusting every Saturday and your roommate lives to scrub the sink, stick with the same jobs, and everything will go smoothly making your room sparkle.

Tip #6 – Duck and Cover

Here are some of the most sensitive issues that can cause conflict, all of which can be addressed when you first talk to your roommate, whether it is on the phone or in person:

- Cleanliness or lack thereof

- Sharing/borrowing/taking personal belongings

- Noise

- Drugs and alcohol

- Views on overnight or frequent guests

- Conflicting sleep and study schedules

- Room temperature/level of light in room

- Different cultural backgrounds

KIM: You want to make a good impression when first meeting your roommate so do not come on too strong or ask too many questions. Go somewhere where you both feel at ease: the campus coffee shop, the food court, or a walk around campus.

Your First Few Days

You have already had a tour of campus and if your parents were with you, what they want you to do the first few days may differ greatly from what you want to do. Your parents may have told you to first go to the on-campus bank and open a checking account, organize your room, lock the door, and then call them every hour to report on your new life. You may want to go to the first party or social gathering your residence hall has to offer. You may want to hit the bookstore first to be sure to get all of your textbooks. Many students I spoke with wanted to map out the buildings their classes would be held in and locate restaurants, places for students to hang out, and find their way around on their own. If you do not already know this, find out what the grace period is for switching rooms. It may be a few weeks into the semester or your university may not have one at all. It is a good thing to know just in case the honeymoon ends sooner than you wanted.

Megan O'Leary-Buda, a residence hall director at Quinnipiac University in Connecticut, writes in "What to Expect When You Arrive at College" (see Appendices), that you want to be sure your ID is in order, and you will want to find out if and where you can deposit money on it to use in the dining hall and around campus. At Temple University, where I work, students and employees can use their ID card as a debit card just about anywhere on campus. Money can be deposited on IDs through an online portal, which is also the main academic resource for class schedules and assignments. Check out the libraries and tech centers as you will be spending a lot of time there. If you have a medical condition, you might want to visit the student health center. If you have food or life-threatening allergies, be sure the health center has your records and up-to-date information on prescriptions. If your phone, cable, or Internet hookups are not included in your housing fees, find out how to get them connected and what kind of service is available.

Most important, this is the time to make a good impression on your roommate. Before you start to notice each other's annoying habits, get to know who this person is: her family, where she is from, her likes, and dislikes. Go for coffee with your laptops and make up a class, work, and guest-visitor schedule so you both have a better understanding of what is ahead should conflict come your way.

> **KIM:** Take time to get acclimated in your dorm and around campus. Enjoy the days before classes by decorating your room, organizing your stuff, buying books and supplies, and getting settled in your new home. Take your roommate for coffee and get to know each other.

Before You Move-In: Getting to Know Your New Roommate

One of the residential professionals I spoke to told me how more incoming students are "researching" their future roommates on MySpace and Facebook. Anyone familiar with the kind of detailed, personal information some people post on these two online diaries will know it is easy to get the scoop on someone's tastes in music, drugs, clothes, and friends. And it is not only the students doing the research; parents, especially the "helicopter" kind (you know how a helicopter hovers), take to the Internet to find out if their perfect 18-year-old will be rooming with a drug dealer with enough body piercings to start a jewelry store.

Note to parents: In addition to discussing the dangers of drugs and unprotected sex with your 18-year-old before you send him off to college, talk to him about the kinds of conflicts he will undoubtedly encounter with his roommates. If your child has not yet developed solid communication and social skills, especially if she tends to be shy, do some role-playing and envision different scenarios, such as sharing or not being respectful of one's study schedule. University-housing Web sites include tips on how to avoid conflict with a new roommate before you move in, as well as tips on roommate conflict resolution. You could even print these out and keep them handy just in case. But we will think positively.

Once you get your roommate assignment, schedule time to talk to that person. That is "talk," not instant messaging (IM) or e-mail. Have an actual conversation with him. You had better learn to do that now, or it is going to be a tense and quiet four years. Do not get into nitty-gritty arrangements during the beginning of the conversation. Get to know him. Talk about expectations, habits, and your life styles and schedules. Discuss who should bring what so you do not have two microwaves and two blenders with space for only one. Talk about furniture arrangements and décor. It is good to know ahead of time what your roommate has in mind for wall hangings, color schemes, rugs, and furniture arrangements. Many universities now have roommate contracts in place so agreements can be put into writing, which makes it a little easier to resolve disagreements later on.

KIM: There is a good reason why the housing-selection form instructs you to take your time in selecting compatible roommates and to consider accommodations that most closely meet your needs. A poor roommate match, based on misinformation from you, is hard to undo.

You May Be Best Friends Now

You have known each other since second grade and spent

more time at each other's homes the past few years than your own. You have called her mother "Mom" since fourth grade. Half of the clothes in your closet belong to her. That is great. Lifelong friendships can be more rewarding and successful than those with your family. But it does not make for a successful relationship as college roommates. Many colleges strongly recommended that you not live with a close friend and may even state this in housing literature.

If you cannot think of why that could possibly be, think about this: One of you gets a boyfriend before the other. He is there often. Your best friend now has less time for you and is hanging the "Come back later, I'm studying" note on the door more often. Here is another: One of you joins a sorority and the other does not. Now you have moved into new realm of social relationships and your soon-to-be-ex-best friend is jealous. If you must be near your best friend in college, live in the same hall, even on the same floor, but not in the same room. If you truly value this relationship and want it to continue until you both qualify for American Association of Retired Persons (AARP) membership, take the time to think about the things that could go wrong. Or, better yet, get caught up on some of the more sensational celebrity divorces. At one time, these people also thought they could not live without each other.

Reasons why rooming with a friend or best friend are not a good idea:

- One of you will get a girlfriend/boyfriend before the other. This may cause the friend to feel like an outsider and create jealousy.

- You are entering a new phase of your life and may outgrow the friendship.

- You will make new friends, which could create a rift between you and your roommate, for whom it may take longer to forge new relationships.

- High school is not college. This is a different world. If you expect college to be an extension of high school, you are in for a big disappointment.

If you were insistent upon rooming with an old friend, and the agreement was mutual, it is likely one of you will move in a different direction, outgrow the friendship, or mature quicker than the other. This will lead to tension and confusion as your friend may be asking herself, "I don't get it. We used to be so close and now we hardly talk to each other any more." You are both experiencing new surroundings, relationships, and a higher level of expectations. All new students are going through a period of adjustment; so do not be too hard on yourself.

If you find yourself in that situation, here are a few tips on how to approach your friend, and now roommate:

- If your old friend is clinging and looking to you to be her only friend and lifeboat as she treads new waters, be honest, but not hurtful, with your feelings:

  "I know things are different now for both of us, but I want this to work. We just need a little space, you know, spend less time together and make new friends."

If she responds that your comments hurt her feelings, be gentle. Think about all the fun experiences you had together before college. You want to respect this friendship, but you want her to be realistic and respect your need to mature and grow.

- If the tension level is high and you are both asking yourselves why you ever thought living together would be a good idea but do not want to abandon the situation, look at the glass as half full, rather than half empty:

  "I know things are tense right now, and we're both experiencing new things, but that doesn't mean we still can't live together."

  Then, have a productive discussion on where the tension lies, what the conflicting issues are and how you can both move forward and remain friends.

If you both get to a point where living together will destroy your friendship, and you both have acknowledged such, it may be time to split and move on to new roommates for the next semester. Hopefully, your friendship has not been permanently damaged and it may even flourish and go the next level by living apart but staying in touch. After all, you have a bond that may go back to first grade, and that is rare in a society that has become more transient and global.

KIM: Longtime friendships can be rewarding throughout your life but do not make for the best-matched roommates. Think about the future value of that relationship before moving in with someone you have known for years.

The First Conversation

It is hard to believe that less than a decade ago, people communicated primarily by phone. That is, they picked up the phone, dialed a number, and had a conversation with someone. Those days are long gone for certain populations, and avoiding it may have worked well for you during your high school years. But if you are going to live in a small space with one or two people you will not know in the beginning, it might be wise to develop some conversation skills, or it is going to be a quiet four years.

This means that it is a good idea (an excellent idea) to have a conversation or two with your new roommate(s) before you move in together. It is all right to make the initial contact via e-mail. But at some point, having a conversation will help you become familiar with his or her voice and mannerisms, which can tell you a lot about someone's personality. Talking to him or her will also mean that the conversation will start itself and go in a direction you had not anticipated. Such dialogue will break the ice so you do not feel like complete strangers the first time you meet.

A student I spoke with, named Marie, met her new roommate for coffee before classes started, since they did not live far from each other. Because the third roommate lived in a different state and had not had a chance to meet them, she later told Marie how left out she felt the first few weeks because the other two had already established a relationship. It may not be possible to arrange, but if you can meet your roommates before school starts, it makes the awkwardness of choosing a bed or meeting new students and their parents easier. Move-in day is hectic and can be stressful, so any strategies you can apply to make that initial transition easier will make the first few days and weeks easier as well.

If you have no idea how to start the conversation, here are a few "starters" to get you going. You do not need to have a script in front of you during the initial conversation, but use these tips as guidelines. You will find the conversation taking its own direction after you share some initial information. Assume each of you has already made initial contact via e-mail and set up time to talk on the phone. (That is the telephone, not via IM or e-mail.)

- "What made you choose X college or university?"

- "What is your major?"

- "Are you ready for move-in day?"

- "What do you like to do in your spare time? I like to . . ."

- "Do you have a nickname?"

- "Tell me about your family"

- "Where did you grow up?"

- "Do you mind going over a list of what we each plan to bring?"

- "I see on your preference form that you run every morning. That's impressive. What time do you usually get up?"

- "I am worried about not being able to ... Are you?"

- "I am really looking forward to … What about you?"

- "Do you plan to work this semester?"

- "I wanted you to know I have a peanut allergy . . ."

- "I tend to get really stressed when it comes to taking tests."

Questions about expectations:

- "Do you think you will study more in the room or the tech lab/library?"

- "Are you all right cleaning the room every week?"

- "If one of us has a guest, how long should they stay? Are you willing to work out an overnight schedule every now and then?"

- "I cannot concentrate with the TV on but you can use headphones."

> **KIM:** Have reasonable expectations about living with a roommate from the start rather than those that cannot possibly be met.

Do You Need to Put It in Writing?

Let's face it: The average incoming freshman will not want to consider a written agreement with her roommate before arriving on campus. She has already completed enough forms and does not want to look like a dork or, even worse, like it was something her parents made her do. But there is a freshman population that is organized by nature, takes academics seriously, and does not want any surprises when they arrive and find themselves completely mismatched with a roommate. This is especially true for undergraduates who will be working in addition to carrying a full class load.

For those students who want to work out details before arriving, an informal negotiating document may be the way to go. Penn State University provides guidelines called "Negotiating a Compromise" that can be used to get an agreement in place before moving in. This document is a good reference point in case conflicts arise after living together, and no agreement was previously put into place. If you want to develop such a document and do not see one already in place, contact your residence director (RD) or residence advisor (RA).

Some of the topics Penn State suggests you include in a written agreement (both generic and specific) include:

- Past experience living with roommates

- Study and sleep habits

- Policy on borrowing personal items

- Agreement on overnight guests and visitors

- Preferred quiet times

- Cleaning schedules and contributing cleaning products

- Preferred room temperature

- Preferred times to receive phone calls

- Preference for windows open and closed

- Music/television volume while studying or not studying

- How often room will be cleaned and splitting costs for products

(See Appendices for Penn State's guidelines, "Negotiating a Compromise.")

If you do not think you are up to creating an agreement form on your own, you can use Penn State's as a guideline to sit down with your roommate and hammer out an informal agreement. You can also find similar agreements on many other university housing Web sites. You may not cover every topic that will come up, but think of it as a "starter" agreement. Both of you can add to it as you get to know each other's likes, dislikes, and living preferences. It would not hurt to revisit it once a semester for updates. Again, this does not have to be a formal agreement, just a document, in writing, on the terms of your living arrangement. Even having such a document in place will not preclude either of you from getting on each other's nerves or encountering conflict. Both of these are not only human nature, but part of living with another person or people in close quarters.

When, or if, the agreement is breached by either one of you, it is always best to address it with tact and honesty. Reiterate to your roommate that the agreement has been breached. Remind him of the part of the agreement that was breached (no sharing of laptops). In other words, do not mince words, be forthright:

"I thought we had an agreement about _____. Did something change without my knowledge?"

"Didn't we agree on _____?"

"I think we need to revisit our agreement as I remember we both said we would not _____."

"Maybe it is time to sit down and renegotiate our agreement."

If your roommate acknowledges the agreement was breached but continues the behavior, bring it up again when neither of you is distracted. Get out a copy of the agreement, get on his calendar, and sit down over his favorite snack and hammer it out. If you need to tweak some of the language, and those changes are all right with both of you, consider it an amended agreement. This is a valuable skill to acquire before you enter the post-college world where negotiation becomes a reality — from employment contracts and loan agreements to prenuptial and divorce agreements to purchasing a car — having the skill to get what you want and showing flexibility and respecting the other person's wants will serve you well.

> **KIM:** Develop a written agreement regarding living arrangements. This can be an informal document that gets revisited every semester or when a conflict calls for a reassessment.

First Homework Assignment: Becoming Acclimated to Residential Living

The best place to start researching the housing-application process, regardless of the university you will attend, is on the university's Web site. Go to just about any university's Web site, type "housing" in the search box, and you will find all the information you need to apply and establish a personalized housing account. Even though you will have an orientation at the beginning of the semester, it is always a good idea to do some homework before the first day of classes.

Examples of information found on most university housing Web sites include:

- Fees, application, deadlines, and contracts

- Hall-selection process (undergraduate versus graduate)

- Roommate-preference forms

- Hall-preference forms

- Room-change requests

- Online tours

- Security and access information

- Policies/code of conduct

- Move-in/move-out deadlines and procedures

- List of things to bring

- Process to select or become a hall group leader

- Hall activities and programs

- Meal plan

- Community-living selections

- Resident-staff listings

- Alternative housing

- Student-employment opportunities

- Information for parents

At larger universities, several buildings may be grouped by area. Each area, or group, will have a name. You can search the area and review each hall within that area. If most of your classes will take place in buildings located in one section of campus, you might want to select a hall near that location. This is especially true at larger universities, where the campus may be sprawling and encompass several square miles.

On most housing Web sites, you can view the amenities of each hall, the number of vacancies, room type (single and double), current occupancy, and priority status. Take advantage of online tours so you can see the actual facility. Here is an example of the information you will find listed for a specific hall or building:

- Name of hall and location

- Number of students and staff per building

- Coed, single-gender suites, singles, doubles, and triples in suites

- Separate coed or single-gender floors within a building

- Common study area

- Single-gender floors

- Mini-suite

- Number of floors

- List of living and learning communities

- Number/location of kitchens or attached cafeterias

Some universities require freshmen to live on campus to help them get acclimated in an environment designed with their needs in mind. At most universities, hall-selection priority is determined by the number of semesters a student has lived on campus. At others, it is a lottery system. Every attempt is made to assign you to the hall or room type you originally requested, but it is all based on space availability and whether you submitted your request before the deadline. If you request a specific roommate, that person must also make a mutual request.

On the university's Web site, you will find antidiscrimination language that states the university will not assign housing or discriminate in assignments based on race, color, religion, gender, national origin, ancestry, age, disability, veteran status, sexual orientation, illness (including human immunodeficiency virus, or HIV, status), arrest or conviction records, perceived socioeconomic status, or perceptions based on personal profiles found on the Internet.

Halls can also be designated by category. For instance, a hall may be designated as "substance-free," "international students," or "all female," so if this is important to you, look for these designations. If you do not see a preference online, contact the housing office.

You should also become familiar with the university's dismissal policies as your behavior, and that of your roommate's, could at some point be at issue. You will find these policies either in the housing agreement you signed or can get a copy online or at the housing office. Be certain you are familiar with first-offense or zero-tolerance behavior which can result in immediate dismissal. Now that you are part of a living community, you are obligated to adhere to policies and have the responsibility of reporting anyone who violates them as he or she could jeopardize the well-being and safety of other dorm mates. Some first offenses may be:

- Possession or intention to use or sell illegal narcotics or firearms

- Throwing or dropping objects from windows or rooftops

- Tampering with fire equipment, security systems or alarms

- Setting fires

- Possession of alcohol or hosting a party where it is served or available to minors

- Assault or battery of another individual

- Hacking into or disrupting university computer networks or systems

- Verbal, physical, or sexual harassment or intimidation

> **KIM:** Take time to browse the university's housing Web site. Most Web sites include pertinent information on deadlines, fees, forms, and policies, and provide contact information, photos, and virtual tours.

To Bring or Not to Bring

The first piece of advice is not to bring everything you own to your dorm. Do not even bring one-half of everything you own. Just like packing for a trip, when you bring something you feel you "simply cannot live without for five days," remember that just about anything you will need at college you will be able to find or buy at college. Unless you are studying abroad, or have special medical needs that require a prescription, even the most remote, private colleges will have resources and access to items you may need but did not bring from home. (If you do require prescriptions, be sure you have the contact information from your pharmacy in case you need to transfer it to one closer to where you are living.) Also, unless you are in an apartment or graduate housing in a single, the space will seem much smaller once you, and possibly two other roommates unpack and get settled.

There are common items you will find already in place in most residence halls, including beds, desks, chairs, mirrors, carpet, a small refrigerator, and closets. If you will be living in a suite, appliances will be there. Some halls will even have a built-in microwave, which means one less thing for you to bring. Other basics you will find in most rooms are Ethernet connections, telephones (often with voice mail), and a TV hookup (cable/digital). Other facilities you will likely find in your hall include laundry facilities, shared kitchens, a game room, community TV/recreational room, study lounges, dining facilities, and a computer lab.

Most universities post an online checklist of "things to bring" or a list of items to coordinate with your roommate, such as coffeemaker, stereo, cooking and eating utensils (if applicable to your living arrangement), and other small furniture items. Pay close attention to this list if your university provides it, because some items may never occur to you, such as an umbrella, first-aid items, basic tools, hangers, envelopes, and postage stamps (to mail the bills for which you are now responsible). If your university does not provide a "what-to-bring list," it should provide you with a list of things not to bring, such as halogen lamps, candles, incense, weapons, pets (some universities allow fish), or open-coil cooking appliances. You will want to review this list carefully, perhaps along with your parents, as you do not want to be known in your hall as "the person who started a fire on her first day."

Megan O'Leary-Buda, residence hall director for off-campus properties at Quinnipiac University in Connecticut, has compiled a concise and useful checklist of items to bring to college. Some of the items she has included may not be the first to come to mind when you are packing, including dishwasher soap, rolls of quarters for laundry, sewing kit, and a shower caddy. Again, most items you may neglect to pack can be purchased on or nearby campus. The full checklist is included in Appendices.

KIM: Bring only what you need. Unless you have special circumstances, you will be able to purchase most personal items on campus or at a nearby store. Also, keep bulky, winter clothes at home if you can easily pick them up before the onset of winter.

The First of Many Forms

You have managed to successfully complete a college application, or you would not be reading this book. However, if your parents completed that for you, shame on them. You need to learn to do these things on your own. Now comes the residency application and preference form. Do not worry. They do not require an essay. You will get enough practice at that over the next four years. What they do require is honesty. This is not the time to be creative or fantasize about the person you always wanted to be. This is the time to be honest about yourself and the type of person you want to room with. One of the university housing officials I spoke with said he is constantly amazed at how students think they will get matched with the ideal roommate by submitting information about themselves that simply is not true.

Universities now require a signed contract from students before they are allowed to select room or hall assignments. Those contracts are found online and can be submitted electronically. They may be considered legal documents. (The contract will state as such.) When you sign a residence hall contract, you understand and agree to the following terms, policies, and procedures, some of which are:

- Terms of the contract (by academic year)

- Obligations: yours, the university's, and joint

- Housing-conduct rules, regulations, and policies

- Rates, payment, deposit, late fees, and rate changes

- Disciplinary action

- Meal plan/food services

- Appeal process

- Liability/damages and associated costs

- Check-in/check-out

- Security, fire, and safety policy for entry into student rooms

- Telephone services

- Internet/cable service and hookup

- Smoking/no smoking

- Vacation periods

- Damage assessment policy and fees

- Cancellation, termination, release, and refunds

Every section of the contract is important, but the "rules and regulations" section may be the longest. This section is more likely to tell you everything you cannot do rather than what you can. Here you will see rules such as where you cannot park a bike, the acceptable wattage of your microwave, the acceptable size of a fish tank, and policies on distributing political-campaign flyers. Read this section carefully, as it will help you narrow down the list of things you were planning to bring.

> **KIM:** Now is a good time to start taking responsibility for choices that directly affect your living situation. It is all right to have your parents read over contractual obligations attached to dorm life, but you should understand the terms and obligations before signing any agreements.

Living Learning Communities (LLC)

Living learning communities provide settings where student academic success is supported through residential experiences. A floor, or section, within a residential hall is specifically designated for students who share common interests or academic majors, and feature programs, social activities, field trips, and other recreational activities that promote the particular community. The staff assigned to the community may be experienced in the area of interest or major, and help students plan programs and activities. That staff person, or others assigned under his or her supervision, can also help new students adjust to university life and answer questions about classes, building locations, policies, and resources. LLCs provide opportunities for students to build strong relationships with peers with whom they share similar interests.

Sharing similar interests on the outset may also reduce

the likelihood of conflicts with your roommates. Although you could still have opposite sleep or study habits, or be in a "neat versus slob" situation, you will at least have the bond of common interests, which could serve as a foundation for constructive dialogue when conflict arises.

Priority for placement within an LLC may be reserved for students enrolled in the academic program affiliated with that community. For example, to live in a performing-arts LLC, you may have to be formally enrolled in a music or dance program. However, there are many LLCs that are not associated with an academic program, such as a "quiet" or "alternative-gender" LLC.

Examples of LLCs are diverse, and there are numerous opportunities to live in a community that fosters student involvement and shared experiences. If you are interested in an LLC and it is not listed on the university's housing Web site, contact the office. There may be a list of other students who are looking for the same LLC as you, and you could be the catalyst for starting a new community.

Many LLCs involve not only RAs and RDs, also but faculty members and local business leaders, who provide individual attention to students seeking career guidance. LLCs can also offer a free professional-speaker series, resume-building workshops, house dinners, and beneficial freebies.

Here is a sample of the kind of diverse LLCs offered at universities around the country:

- By major: architecture, music, forensic science, and engineering

- Community service

- Social justice

- French- and Spanish-speaking communities

- Cross-cultural education

- Global living

- Outdoor adventure

- Rainbow House (gay, lesbian, bisexual, transgender)

- Chicano/Latino cultural studies

- Black/African-American scholars

- Women in science and technology

KIM: If your schedule allows, take advantage of the cultural, educational, and social opportunities offered through and at your residence hall (and university). Being involved will enrich your college experience and increase the likelihood of making new friends.

Students with Disabilities, Special and Medical Needs, and International Students

The housing office works in conjunction with the office of disability services to offer options for students requiring disability-related housing accommodations. Wheelchair access and other barrier-free spaces can be arranged upon request, and universities have separate printed guidelines available in the office.

Universities host students from hundreds of countries each year and have designated departments, offices, and staff to assist international students in getting acclimated to their new country, university, and home away from home. Most residence halls welcome both American and international students while others may have designated buildings or floors just for foreign students.

If you have any food allergies, you should have contacted the university even before applying to be certain their food-services operations can accommodate your needs, including a specially designed menu and segregated eating areas, especially for peanut allergies. Be sure to tell your roommate about any food allergies. If you use an EpiPen, show your roommate where you keep it and explain to him or her how to use it in case of an emergency.

The number of young people and college students who suffer from asthma and allergies has increased dramatically over the past decade. Small living quarters, mold, and dust mites trigger allergy symptoms and, for some students, lend to a life-threatening living environment. Students suffering from allergies should contact the housing office at their university well in advance of the application process to find out what its policy is on allergy-proof rooms. They must also be absolutely certain they are not matched with a smoker or a roommate who may not smoke, but socialize in smoke-filled venues at which smoke will be absorbed in their clothing. Many times, the school will be able to accommodate their needs but they must act early. Dorms that have central air pose less of a problem, but if the university needs to accommodate special needs, early contact is crucial. It is also advisable that students check in with health services upon arrival so they have a record of their medical needs. Another resource may be the university's office of disabilities. If you use an inhaler or other asthma medication, show your roommate where you keep it and be sure he or she is aware of your condition should you need emergency help.

The Allergy and Asthma Network Mothers of Asthmatics (**www. aanma.org**) posts helpful information for college-bound students on how to navigate dorm living. It suggests students with asthma obtain an updated, written management plan from his or her allergist before leaving for college. It also suggests that dorm rooms are clutter free, with no upholstered furniture or secondhand rugs, an air filter, encased bedding, and regularly scheduled vacuuming and dusting. Asthmatic students and their parents should also know the location of the nearest hospital.

KIM: Your university should be able to accommodate any special needs if you have investigated available resources ahead of time. Investigating available services should be on your list when first shopping for colleges.

2

Once You Are There

Claiming Your Territory

Have you ever watched *The Real World*? If not, you might want to view a few episodes — not only to see what the most obnoxious roommate on the face of the planet looks like, but also to see him claim the first bed he sees without consulting anyone else. This is even before introductions are made. Not a good way to make friends.

The hope is that you will be assigned reasonable roommates who understand that compromise plays a major role in getting along, and this includes that moment when everyone claims his or her space. If you do not care where your bed is, say so right away. This will make it easier for a roommate who may have particular reasons why she wants a bed near the door or against the wall. Just like living with your family, everyone will have their quirks.

Wait until everyone is in the room and after introductions are made. If possible, wait until parents have said their good-byes so they are not part of the decision-making. Also, whichever space you claim is not a permanent decision. You can come up with a schedule to alternate spaces every semester or year. This is not Buckingham Palace. You have approximately 10 X 10 feet to work with. Also, if you brought an item that will not fit in your room or closet, ask your parents to bring it back home.

Megan, a second semester freshman and the University of Massachusetts, told me that she and her roommates (she had two) decided who would get which bed and which closet a few weeks before moving in. It saved them a lot of trouble, especially when they heard about the arguments between hall mates over who claimed what and when.

To best use what will become a space more cramped than it is when you first move in, plan to use your closet to hold as many items as possible. You want to do this for two reasons: so you can find what you need quickly and so that you are not tossing your clothes, shoes, and anything else on the floor or on your roommate's bed. Dorm closets are small. Yours may have just a rod without any doors, sliding doors, or shutter-type doors that open out. Over-the-door hooks and shelves are great space savers and do not require any holes, screws, or nails. Collapsible, folding shelves are another great space saver since floor space is minimal. They are five feet high and less than two feet square. You can use them to store textbooks, bike equipment, and beauty and health items. To even better utilize shelf space, buy some stacking trays. They come in various sizes and some lift up or slide out like drawers.

When it comes to décor, well, this is a tough one. Unless you paint a white line dividing the room in half, or unless you are lucky enough to be living in a suite with your own bedroom, you will be subject to your roommate's tastes in wall hangings, plants, rugs, lamps, and everything else that may not appeal to your better sense of style. They will have to endure the same from you.

Benita grew up in New York and went to a good high school with a diverse student body. She selected a private, woman's college in Massachusetts because it offered a recognized program in her major, but she also wanted to get away from the city for a few years. After she got settled on move-in day and said goodbye to her parents, she walked around campus, as her roommate had not yet arrived. She wanted to wait until they were both introduced before selecting a bed so she left her bags on the floor. When Benita came back, both beds were covered with bags, backpacks, books, and other belongings.

Claiming your Territory: A Story

When her roommate, Rachel, arrived, Benita introduced herself and knew immediately that making this relationship work was going to take some effort. Rachel was dressed in head-to-toe Goth with lots of piercings and wearing chunky black boots, torn black fishnets, a long black skirt, and a black military-style jacket. Her hair was green and jet black and was styled in a semi Mohawk. While Benita had gone to high school with students who dressed like this, she had not been friends with them so did not associate any personality traits with the way they dressed.

Rachel immediately claimed one of the beds and while Benita really did not care one way or the other, she was a bit taken aback by the way Rachel took over. She told Benita she hoped she wasn't going to decorate the room like a Pottery Barn catalog and proceeded to criticize the way women dressed on campus and how they all looked like J. Crew models, which made Benita wonder what Rachel was doing there. Benita decorated her side of the room with many of the colorful fabric designs her mother, who was a designer, had made. Rachel not only told Benita how ugly they were, but had decorated her part of the room mostly in black with crucifixes and images representing death. Many of Benita's friends did not want to come to her room because they thought Rachel was weird and the room depressing.

Neither of them socialized at all the first semester, and Benita spent as much time out of the room as she could. It was not just the way Rachel had decorated, but it was the way she criticized Benita's friends and her negative attitude that eventually convinced her to seek out a new roommate. She could not switch until the following fall, so her first year was a lesson in tolerance and how opposites just cannot get along.

KIM: Do not toss your belongings on a bed and claim it as "yours" the minute you walk into your dorm room. Be open to compromising with your roommates, and remember that you can always switch spaces every semester.

In The Know

In addition to getting acclimated on campus and in your dorm, you will want to navigate your way around campus and become familiar with location of class buildings, cafeterias, food courts, coffee shops, libraries, the tech center, bank, and bookstore. You also should know what services are provided by and within your dorm and what you need to provide or do on your own. It has been a few months since you read that housing contract so here are some important questions to find answers to as you settle in during the first few days:

- What is the trash disposal/recycling policy?

- When is trash picked up?

- Does the dorm provide trash bags?

- What happens if I neglect to properly dispose trash at curbside? Is there a fine?

- Where can I store my bike?

- Do I need to move my car during snow removal?

- Does the university provide long-distance phone service if I do not have my own? If so, how can I get it?

- Is my room cable- and Internet-ready? If not, how do I get them connected?

- Can I get a satellite dish installed?

- What kind of laundry services are available? Is the cost included in my housing fee?

- What are the evacuation procedures?

- What happens if damage is done to my room or on my dorm floor? What am I responsible for?

- What happens if damage occurs but it is an accident?

This is also a good time to review the noise, overnight-guest, and prohibited-behavior sections of your housing contract.

What About Me?

How much of the college experience is about you? All of it, you say? If your parent(s) are paying for any portion of your college tuition, room, and board, then much is about them. Also, think about how difficult it is for your parent(s) to see you go. Just because they turned your room into a fitness center the moment you sent in that acceptance letter does not mean they do not miss you. That is their way of sending you a valuable message, which is:

You are no longer the center of the universe. You are an adult now, with adult responsibilities.

You may be thinking: What? How can that possibly be? I thought college was all about partying, staying up late, drinking, having sex, and wearing my pajamas to class. You mean there will be responsibilities like the ones my parents have? I did not bargain for this.

Living with roommates is like being in a relationship. You have to take the bad with the good. These people will have their annoying habits, but so do you. You will not be able to have everything your way and will have to find a fair balance that allows your rights to be respected and heard as well as theirs.

You will encounter students, whether in or outside your residence hall, who act like it is still high school. This is especially common when a group of high school graduates go to a local college and assume everything will be the same except they will be living in a different place and have more freedom. While it is not frowned upon to maintain friendships from high school, do not expect those relationships to be the same as they were. You are in a larger and more diverse environment. You will want, and are encouraged to, expand your circle of friends. This will happen on its own, without effort. You will begin to socialize with students who have the same major as you do or you may join a fraternity, sorority, or other club. This is all part of expanding your circle of friends, growing socially, and maturing into a responsible adult.

While moving away from home and living independently of their family may sound intimidating to some, many others cannot wait for the opportunity. But for even the bravest of souls, homesickness is more common than rare. Unless you are an international student, almost everyone is able to go home on weekends or holidays. It is a nice balance between real adulthood and the security of the home you have known for 18 years where you can still sleep in, and Mom will still make your favorite French toast and do your laundry. But then it is time to face the real world and always keep in mind that you have responsibilities that belong to only you, and Mom and Dad cannot be there to help you find your way.

KIM: Part of the experience of leaving home and living on your own is to realize that you have to accept other people's faults and personalities. By doing so, you will be better prepared for post-college professional and personal relationships.

R-E-S-P-E-C-T

Picture Aretha Franklin belting out this song. She is a woman in charge and I do not know about you, but I do not want to mess with her. She demands "respect." The same goes with mutual expectations of your roommate and yourself. You should respect his space, privacy, belongings, life style, and desire to get the best education he can. He should do the same for you. If all roommates followed this guideline, there would be no reason for me to write this section, as everyone would be respectful of everyone else.

Here are some of the most common claims of disrespect I heard from a group of third- and fourth-year students, and how they were resolved:

- *He doesn't respect my wish to study.* He thinks college is one giant party, but my parents have shelled out tens of thousands of dollars for me to go here. I am transferring next semester to an honors dorm where students take studying seriously.

- *She doesn't respect the fact that this is my room, too.* She rotates boyfriends and thinks I don't know they're having sex when I'm in class or at work. I can't tell you how many times I came home and my bed was a mess. I've complained to my RD and she's being reassigned to a different floor.

- *He doesn't respect my right to peace and quiet.* Evidently, my roommate has never heard of headsets. He said he likes the "full effect" of hearing music blasted all day through a giant set of speakers. I will study in the library or in a friend's room, but why should I always have to accommodate him? I complained to the RD and he now must wear a headset when listening to music. He's not happy with me, but frankly, I don't care.

- *She doesn't respect my things.* My roommate assumes it is all right to use my shampoo, soap, and hair products. I don't know where she got this from because we actually set up a written agreement at the beginning of the year that neither of us wanted to share our things. The first time I pointed this out to her, she laughed at me. When I locked my shampoo in my closet, she had the nerve to ask me where it was. I told her I had run out and that she would have to buy her own. When she saw it in the shower the next day, after she bought her own, she got the message.

- *He doesn't respect my political (religious) beliefs.* I'm a Christian and get up early every morning to pray. Sometimes a group of us on the floor pray in the game room while everyone is still sleeping. I'm not bothering my roommate, but he makes fun of my "God groupies." I don't know what his religious preference is but I told him that his jokes aren't funny and they not only hurt my feelings, but insult my family. When I asked him how he would feel if someone insulted his family that put an end to his remarks. Now when I joke and ask him if he'd like to join our group, we both have a good laugh.

Accepting that you will have to adjust your attitude somewhat to mesh with the person you live with should not come as a surprise. After all, you did the same thing with your parents and siblings, even though you may not have verbalized it as such. When you took something that belonged to your sister or when you made fun of her or her friends, you were showing signs of disrespect. There is a good chance you were reprimanded and perhaps even suffered some consequences of your behavior. Your parents might even have said to you, "This house is not yours and yours only," or, "Those are your sister's friends and they deserve your respect, as does your sister." The old adage about treating those as you would like them to treat you holds true when it comes to respecting the person (or people) you room with. Think about how you want to be treated, and treat them, their belongings and life style in the same way.

> **KIM:** Your roommate and you have the right to have your belongings, living environment, pursuit of an education, and life style mutually respected.

Most Common Complaints

Talk to a university housing director, and she will give you a list of the most common complaints roommates have about each other that is universal, whether it is an East Coast, West Coast, private, or urban university. The commonalities have little to do with the university or college itself, but with the realities of living in a small space with other human beings who initially are strangers. We will examine each of these in detail in the following chapter, but here is the list, in no particular order:

- Different sleep and study habits

- Hygiene (or lack thereof)

- Cleanliness

- Respect for others' belongings

- Overnight guests

- Substance use

- Mental health issues

- Differences in cultural background, sexual orientation, and religious beliefs

- Room temperature (battles over thermostat)

- Noise levels

Here are two insightful tips gleamed from experienced resident assistants when it comes to potential roommate conflict:

- If you end up with a roommate who leads a wild existence and could care less about getting a college education, be assertive. Move into an honors dorm or get on a waiting list for a single. One of the biggest conflicts I have seen and heard about is when two people are completely mismatched when it comes to study habits. You may have a computer science major who is serious about his chosen path rooming with an undeclared freshman who has no intention of declaring a major anytime soon because partying is just too much fun. Take the lead and create change on your own.

- If you find yourself with a new roommate every semester, take a good, deep look at yourself. Maybe you are the problem. Maybe you are difficult to live with and always blame the other person. Think about a thread to the reasons roommates moved out. Did they share anything with you that leads you to believe you have to change some things and be more flexible? If you are the one moving from dorm to dorm, perhaps you have set up unrealistic expectations of what a roommate relationship is like. If you are looking for the perfect relationship and someone who matches your personality to a "T," you are no more likely to find it on a college campus than in real life.

> **KIM:** You will, at some point during your tenure as a college student, have a complaint about your college roommate. Many complaints can be easily dealt with by having an immediate conversation rather than assuming the problem will go away on its own. Communication is the key to a successful roommate experience.

Do Opposites Attract?

Sometimes, yes, other times, no way. If you and your roommate have similar schedules, are both neat (or sloppy) but have different majors, interests, and friends, that could be the formula for a successful relationship. Think about it: you have the same friends, like the same music, share interests, and are spending a lot of time together. The result? Friendship burn out is one. Another common problem is that a third party comes along, such as a girlfriend or new "best friend." Jennifer, a third-year student at the University of Delaware, told me that she immediately clicked with her roommate freshman year. They felt like they were playing the roles of the twins in the movie, "The Parent Trap," constantly discovering similarities in their lives and life styles. At first, this seemed like a plus. Then Jennifer joined a sorority in her second semester and her roommate became jealous and accused Jennifer of abandoning their friendship when in reality, Jennifer was just hanging out with new people and spending more time away from her dorm room. She never had a plan to change who she was and could keep her friendships separate. Even while she was exploring new relationships through her sorority, she still enjoyed spending time with her roommate. It was her roommate who needed reassurance that Jennifer was still "the same old Jennifer."

If you embellished a bit on the roommate-preference forms and portrayed yourself as the complete opposite of who you really are, does it matter? Are you the type of person who does not see a problem with stashing stale pizza crusts under your bed but noted on the form that you are tidy and neat? Or are you tidy and neat, noted that on the form, but end up matched with a roommate who leaves nail clippings in the sink and only does his laundry when he has run out of clean underwear? Some students think that if they lie about being tidy, when they have never set foot in the same room as a vacuum cleaner, they will get matched with someone who cleans up for both of them just to avoid living in a swamp.

We are attracted to people because they possess personality traits or talents that we covet. If it is difficult for you to mingle at a social event where you do not know anyone, you may well gravitate toward people who can walk into a room full of strangers and make small talk. It is also possible that you could acquire that particular trait by spending time with people who are naturally outgoing, just as it is possible you could pick up someone's accent by default because you are around him or her every day. There can be positive attributes to being around someone with opposite personality traits.

But if the clash is deeply rooted, based on such things as religious beliefs or political views, and these issues surface on a regular basis, you will not be able to resolve these differences. Someone can hold deep religious beliefs and keep them private, or someone can discuss their beliefs at every opportunity. There is a big difference, and that difference can make or break a successful roommate relationship. If you find yourself at the end of your roommate's personality spectrum, and it is causing ongoing disruption in your daily life, seek out your RD for help. Your roommate may be feeling the same way. A move is necessary to ensure academics are the focus of your college experience, rather than roommate conflict.

> **KIM:** Opposite personalities, life styles, and backgrounds can teach you about a way of life different from your own, expand personal growth, and help develop new friendships.

Your Parents

It is move-in day. You may find that your parents have the urge to panic because they have been raising you for the last 18 years. It can be difficult for them to let you move into the next phase of your life. Reassure them not to worry (they will anyway). Tell them that you will be among new peers and will have the opportunity to make new friends (some they will love and some they will hate). Deep in their hearts, they know that they have to let you go, but even so, this can be difficult for them. To see it from their perspective: They have always been there to hold your hand and protect you from the evils of the world. Now, they have to trust you to make those decisions, and that can be scary because they do not want anything bad happening to you.

You are most likely experiencing many emotions at once. You may want to be close to home but push your parents away at the same time. While you may be sad about leaving the home you have known for 18 years, you will also be excited about new adventures and opportunities. You may want reassurance that your parents will always be there for you, but independence calls. You will likely "brush-off" your parents at your college orientation after you arrive and move in your dorm, and this may make them feel hurt and alone. Remember that they will likely be sad and may take their time leaving. This is a new experience for them also.

Your parents will likely want to be involved with your college career, after all, they are the ones most likely paying tuition and should have some say in your education. However, they should not be making every decision in your life. You may have to compromise with them on some things, but remember that you are your own person and capable of making decisions, too. While your dad may really want you to be a doctor, that might not be the right course for you. Explain to him why you would excel at being a teacher and why pre-med is not the major for you.

I spoke with several housing directors who told me horror stories of parents choosing courses, researching potential roommates online, and visiting dorms before their child was even accepted at that university. Some completed all the paperwork on their child's behalf. Let your parents know that this is a disservice to you because they are not letting you take responsibility and learn to deal with the college experience.

Check the Web site of the university you are attending. Many have dedicated portions of the student-housing or orientation pages to parents, offering tips on contact information, getting adjusted to life on campus, and defining a parent's role when conflict with a roommate arises. Directing your parents to these pages may reassure them and help them help you.

Your parents may call the university during your tenure and try to get more information about you. This could be because they feel you have grown apart from them or that you are not telling them everything. They may call to try to get various types of information, such as your academic, medical, and mental-health records. Often, parents feel that they have the right to do this, especially if they are the ones paying your tuition.

However, there are federal mandates in place to protect your rights. After all, FERPA, the Family Educational Rights Protection Act, gave them the right to inspect these records up until you turned 18 years old. However, when you turned 18, these rights were then transferred to you.

KIM: Your parents may think they have every right to see and know about your academic, medical, and mental-health records while you are in college, especially if they are paying tuition. However, there are federal mandates that protect the rights of college students – even against their parents.

While your parents cannot obtain your records from your college, the school can tell them director information, which contains your name, address, phone number, dates of attendance, honors and awards, and date and place of birth. While you may not think this is a lot of information, your parents can learn a great deal about you this way. For one, if you dropped out, they will easily know. Also, they can see if you were on the Dean's list. This may not seem of a particular interest to you, but consider this: To get on the Dean's list, you need at least a 3.0 GPA. You made a C in a class one semester, causing your GPA to drop under a 3.0. They will know you made a bad grade, even though they will not know what the grade was or the class you made it in. They can start assuming multiple scenarios about you, all of which may be worse than the actual situation, such as you failed a class, or multiple classes.

Case in point, you need to be honest with your parents. They are concerned and in a new situation, just like you. They love you and want to know what is going on in your life. Make sure to include them and give them updates about what is going on in your life. Sit down and discuss your life with them, whether things are positive or negative. This will make them happy that you are communicating with them, and it will likely relieve stress for both you and your parents.

"Mom, Dad, I know it seems like I've been distant lately, but I want you to know that everything in my life is fine. I've been elected Treasurer of the student body and I'm making A's and B's this semester."

"Mom, Dad, I want you to know that I've really been struggling in English. I've tried to get help, but I think I might fail the class. Don't worry, I will be able to retake the course next semester and will work my schedule to devote more time to the course since I know it will give me trouble."

"Mom, Dad, things have been really busy for me, but college is great. I'm having a lot of fun meeting new people and trying new activities. I joined a sorority and the girls are wonderful. They've really helped me get adjusted to the college life."

"Mom, Dad, I've changed my major to journalism. I couldn't handle the pressure of all the chemistry classes I had to take to be pre-med, and my English instructor told me that I have a gift for writing. I want to use that gift to share information with people and tell them what is going on in the world."

MEMORANDUM

To: Mom and Dad

From: Your loving child

Re: Top Ten Tips on What You Should Not Think, Act Upon, or Believe During
            My First Semester at College

#1   Do not call me on my cell phone every hour, leave messages, and then
        worry I've been kidnapped by aliens because your calls are not immediately
        returned.

#2   Voice mail is history. Everyone text messages these days.

#3   Do not text message me every hour. See #1 above.

#4   I will not have sex, take drugs, and drink while naked on the roof of my dorm,
        no matter what Uncle Matt tells you. Anyway, you should be enjoying your
        new-found freedom by converting my room into the yoga studio you always
        wanted.

#5   Do not grill my roommate on my whereabouts, behavior, or social life.

#6   That's because I want to be liked and make friends.

#7   If you don't respect #5 and #6, I'll end up living on the streets or back at home
        in my old room that you converted to a yoga studio.

#8   You know how a helicopter hovers over something, staying up there in the air
        for a really long time? Just wanted to be certain you understood the definition
        of "helicopter."

#9   I promise you will never see me in a "Girls Gone Wild" video, no matter how
        much cash or tequila the producers throw at me.

#10 I love you.

Dorm Staff and How They Can Help

Resident directors, assistants, and hall staff are there to make your experience as positive as they can. While they are obligated to follow and implement policies and guidelines (many of which they helped to develop) they are there to assist you, answer questions and, most of all, ensure your safety and well-being while living in their dorm. Talk to them about conflict. Not only do they have experience as a college roommate, but they live in your dorm and have firsthand experience with conflict and common issues. Take advantage of their expertise and think of them as a valuable resource. Do not go to hall mates first and discuss the problem. That is unfair to your roommate and can make the situation worse.

The housing staff that lives in your residence hall may have different titles but share the responsibilities of overseeing day-to-day operations. Resident directors, "RDs," supervise other staff and are responsible for life within your residence community, overseeing matters related to facilities, and assisting residents when there is a problem. Directors hold either a master's degree or are pursuing a graduate degree. They are supervised by someone who works directly within the housing office and who has professional experience in residence-hall management.

RDs monitor activities and events taking place within your residence hall and enforce the code of conduct. Directors also supervise the resident assistants, or RAs, those individuals who live on each floor. Assistant area coordinators and area coordinators are also full-time, live-in professional staff members in supervisory positions. They are all a valuable resource for students. They know the campus inside out and can help get you acclimated and find your way, both as a student and resident of the university community.

Desk assistants are student workers who man the 24-hour front desks and are responsible for checking ID cards, signing in guests, and answering phones. When there is a 3 a.m. emergency, this is the person you would call or go to. Some universities also have resident-hall governments, which are organizations that encourage students to apply leadership skills and develop a productive and active community environment in the dorm.

You should only take a problem beyond the dorm staff when they have not been able to offer a viable solution. This would mean going to the director of housing or the vice president for student affairs.

> **KIM:** The dorm staff is there to make your time on campus as problem-free as possible, yet they are trained in conflict resolution and are well versed with the complex issues facing college students.

Other Sources of Help

Although the higher level of dorm staff, including the RD and RA, are trained in emergency protocol and recognizing serious mental-health and medical concerns, they are not trained as professional doctors or counselors. As you will read later on, there are myriad mental-health issues facing today's college students, many of which can be debilitating, life threatening, and disruptive to your daily life. While the dorm staff is always a good place to start should your roommate display signs of depression, an eating disorder, or substance abuse, seeking their advice may put you in compromising position, especially if the matter could result in your roommate's expulsion or her knowledge that you have breached her trust.

Student health and student counseling services are good starting places to get information to better educate yourself on a roommate's situation, if it is above and beyond the day-to-day annoyances that are bound to arise. A trusted professor can also provide not only advice, but direction on how to help a roommate in a crisis or one who cannot, for various reasons, help herself.

In the case of an emergency during which your safety or that of your roommate is of concern, the person staffing the front desk on a 24-hour basis is the first one to call. If that person cannot respond quickly enough, call campus security or 911.

KIM: Even though the dorm staff provides the first line of defense when there is a roommate problem or conflict, student health and counseling services or even a professor can also provide some valuable insight.

3

Roommate Survival Skills 101

Let us imagine you are stranded on a desert island (the "why" is not necessary to make the following points). You know a rescue boat is on its way. Your BlackBerry and laptop are keeping the sharks company somewhere off the coast of the Bahamas. It is just you, some loud birds, and shady trees. You are bored out of your mind and feel that without any technological device, life is not worth living. But then you remember that in your pocket is a small guidebook, wrapped in plastic, titled "College Roommate Survival Skills." Let us also assume that you are starting college in two weeks and have not yet made any overtures to reach out to your roommates, whose contact information you have had since June.

You pull the guidebook out of your pocket. It is a bit soggy, but still legible. You review the table of contents and are surprised at some of the topics covered. You ask yourself, "Do people really need to be reminded to shower every day? Don't all students like to study to classic rock?" Here is a quick list of survival skills... for college roommates, that is. You are on your own when it comes to getting off the island.

- Hygiene counts.

- You may fall in love at some point, but that does not mean your roommate feels the same way. Work out overnight arrangements *before* you work them out with the love of your life.

- Do not use the floor as your personal recycling area. Put dirty clothes and smelly sneakers in a container. Put food waste in the trash can.

- Empty the trash can on a regular basis.

- If you did not pay for it, do not assume it is yours. Work out a sharing agreement *before* you eat those chips or "borrow" some shampoo.

- Do not room with your best friend from high school. It is not high school any more.

- Do not assume you can drink or do drugs because you are in college. Some people go to college to learn.

- If your roommate is not a fellow substance abuser, it is not all right to use substances. Period. Plus, you can get expelled from your residence hall. Think about that conversation with your parents before doing anything foolish.

- If you are having a problem with a roommate who takes a nap at 10 p.m. and then studies until dawn, and you did not indicate on your preference form that you are an early riser, even though there was a check box for that, well, Houston, we have a problem.

Do not share purchases you make after moving in. Think of it as a prenuptial agreement ... do you want to have to split a houseplant in two if things do not work out?

KIM: If you are sharing food and other items, keep a running tab posted where everyone can add to and see it.

Hygiene Primer

No one wants to admit he or she could be the problem when it comes to hygiene or lack thereof. We are all of the human species. We are not made of plastic and have to come to terms with the fact that we live with other humans, and humans have body odor, bad breath, stinky feet, smelly clothes, and gross habits, like flossing while your roommate is eating dinner. It is a way of life.

However, when you are sharing a cramped space with one, sometimes two other people, poor or excessive hygiene (think strong perfume) can cause insurmountable tension, hurt feelings, and resentment that can lead to a total breakdown in communication.

The best way to avoid having to deal with this issue is to follow some basic, common-sense guidelines:

Keep Your Body Clean

This may seem like a no-brainer, but unless you are in a single room or too sick to get to the shower, you should bathe every day. It is not just about you anymore. Perhaps your family tolerated your natural scent because they are related to you and love you no matter what, but roommates do not exhibit unconditional love.

It is also about respect. You want to respect the other person's space in the same way you expect them to respect yours.

Wash Your Clothes

When you lived at home, maybe you could heap your dirty clothes on the bedroom floor until you could not navigate past them to access your laptop; but again, unless you live in a single, there will not be room (or tolerance) for any mountain-like structures in residence halls. If you commute home on the weekends and Mom welcomes dirty laundry (and you, of course) with open arms, keep it in a laundry bag until then. Even a large trash bag will do if you can stash it in your closet or in a corner.

Not only can dirty clothes smell from "dirt," but if you have been in a bar or at a party where people are smoking, and you room with someone who is allergic to cigarette smoke, this poses a problem. You may not notice it, but your clothes will smell of smoke. Be considerate and put them in a bag until you can get to a washing machine.

You Are the Only One Who Loves Your Perfume

If you have left the room in the morning but can smell your perfume upon returning eight hours later, you may want to cut back before your roommate has to tell you to. For some reason, people who wear overpowering perfume are the last people to notice it.

Good Environmental Hygiene

You smell like a freshly picked daisy every day. Your clothes sparkle and your hair shines. There is only one problem: Your room is dirty. Dust, dirt particles, food crumbs, hair in the sink, splatters on the mirror, and God only knows what is growing in the sink. Add all these elements together, and you are talking germs. Germs can cause illness, especially for someone with allergies or environmental sensitivities. Share cleaning responsibilities. One week, you vacuum and dust, and the next week, you scrub the sink and wipe down the windowsills. Unless you are in a single unit, you need to remember that this is not your exclusive space.

KIM: Do not assume that because you are now on your own you do not have to take responsibility for good hygiene. If you want to make new friends, and keep them, take care of your body, clothes, and surroundings.

Early Riser Versus Late Sleeper

All right. This potential conflict is one of the most important reasons why it is important to be truthful on your roommate-preference questionnaire. If you have planned your schedule so that all of your classes take place early in the day, but your roommate, who works at night, has scheduled his classes for late morning/early afternoon, someone is not going to get the sleep he or she needs.

You will not always have control over your class schedule, and it will most likely fluctuate from semester to semester. If you are both (or all three) in different class, work, and study "time zones," flexibility, understanding, and patience need to take top priority to keep things running smoothly for all of you.

If you are able, work out a rotating schedule. If John is up at 6 a.m. to study before an early class and you did not get home from work until 11:30 the night before, perhaps he could study in the lounge or the library in the morning so you can get enough sleep. However, accommodating Dan's schedule gets a bit tricky. Even if he spends some time in the lounge after work, he will eventually have to come back to the room late at night. Even if he is as quiet as a mouse, it is likely he will wake you up. Add a third roommate and the situation gets even more challenging.

In this situation, there are two opposite class and sleep schedules. Both John and Dan get along, are good students, and do not want their varied schedules to interfere with their living arrangement. A few tactics to work around this dilemma are:

- Buy earplugs. Seriously. Pilots, flight crews, and business travelers use them all the time in hotels to drown out street noise, especially in major cities.

- In addition to earplugs, buy a sleeping mask. They have come a long way since the one Grandma used to own. Some even contain soothing eye gel. You can get a good night's sleep and ward off wrinkles at the same time.

- Split the cost on a white-noise or sounds-of-nature machine. When your roommate comes in late and you have an early class, you will not even notice because you were serenaded by the soothing sounds of falling rain or a bubbling fountain.

- See if John, the early riser, can schedule later classes if his major allows. This does not help Dan because he cannot change his work schedule. When a student works during college, it is probably because he or she needs to, not because he or she wants to, so John needs to be empathetic to Dan's schedule.

- If this becomes, or remains, a source of ongoing conflict and you know the situation will not change the following year or the year after, discuss whether one of you should volunteer to move in with another roommate who has a similar schedule. This is a last resort because your new roommate could have a schedule agreeable with yours one semester but then not the next.

- Learn to live with it. If things are otherwise good between you and your roommate and you have heard horror stories from friends about students who jumped from one roommate to the next, you could end up with the roommate from hell rather than one whose only fault was to get up early for class.

> **KIM:** You cannot always control your class schedule, so yours may conflict with your roommate's. If your relationship is fine otherwise, try to work out a compromise that allows both of you to get the sleep you need.

Noise Is Just That

I happen to be sensitive to noise. Sniffling, gum snapping, foot shuffling, and loud chewing grate on my nerves. Other people I know could sit between the brass and percussion sections in a full orchestra and take a nap or read a chemistry textbook (and pass the exam the next day).

It is highly likely that you will, at some point, live with a roommate who keeps the TV on all day or considers blasting classic rock a study tool. All of the housing officials I spoke with included "noise" as a cause of conflict between roommates. Most preference questionnaires include a section on whether the student prefers complete quiet, low music, loud music, or television while studying. If you are sensitive to noise or are certain you do not want to live with someone who prefers loud music or television, it would not hurt, when you get to this section, to write a note emphasizing your preference, stating this is an important issue for you. Many dorms also have quiet floors and living learning communities may also have such designated floors as well. If you are an honors student, it may be worth your while to investigate the honors dorm where students take classes and studying more seriously than others.

Some people are just naturally loud — their voice, their mannerisms, due to the surroundings in which they grew up. Some people may not be "loud" but create annoying noise, that is, talk constantly on their cell phone without regard to anyone around them or play their MP3s at such a high volume that a person ten feet away can hear it outside the headphones. As our society becomes more reliant on communicating via cell phone, it has become more culturally acceptable to hold a personal conversation, without lowering your voice, on a train sitting next to someone who is not the least bit interested in what you are having for dinner or which bar you will be at Friday night. On one hand, technology has greatly improved our quality of life. On the other, it has hindered the development of social skills and etiquette for an entire generation.

Noise is Just That: A Story

Sandra is a biology major. She has a 4.0 and needs to get her undergraduate degree in four years as her scholarship money will run out. Studying is serious business to her, as is sleeping. She requested a quiet living arrangement and also attached a note reiterating how important this is to her. Meg, her roommate, is undeclared. She did not care about the roommate questionnaire but thought it would be funny if her younger brother completed it. He checked all the items that were the opposite of Meg's personality, such waking up early (she does not), prefers no noise in her room (her favorite band is The White Stripes), and prefers an alcohol-free environment (everyone who knows Meg knows she cannot wait to drink at college). Matching Sandra with Meg was a formula for disaster. Meg wanted the television on even when she slept. She had headphones and an MP3 player, but insisted on playing CDs in the stereo at full volume. Other floor mates had complained about her, and Sandra was beside herself. The "noise issue" became a conflict the day they both moved in. Sandra tried to talk to Meg about it and explained that she was serious about her classes and could not concentrate with so much noise. Meg told her "too bad," and said if she (Sandra) did not like it, she could move.

Well, it was Meg who did the moving. Their RD was strict about enforcing the noise rule and had warned Meg several times to have the television on only during mutually agreeable times and wear headphones when listening to music. Meg was moved to another dorm and the same problem ensued. She was then asked to leave the dorms and the housing office helped her find an apartment off campus. Even though the solution would not have robbed Meg of her music (using the headset) or the television (watching less but still able to watch), she wanted things her way.

If you find yourself living with a noisemaker who is disturbing your ability to sleep, study, or feel "at home" in your dorm, ask yourself if your expectations are reasonable. If your roommate chews with his mouth open, it is not reasonable to ask him to stop, even though it annoys you.

But if your roommate cannot fall asleep without the television on, ask him to buy headsets and remind him, gently, of your dorm's noise policy. He may not even be aware it is a problem.

> **KIM:** If you live with a noisy roommate, choose which battle is worth fighting. Maybe her gum snapping drives you up a wall, but your constant sniffling, of which you are unaware, makes her want to buy you a truckload of tissues. Do your best to approach the issue in a gentle, noninsulting way.

When Guests Overstay Their Welcome

Sooner or later, and most likely it will be sooner, a new girlfriend or boyfriend will come along, or an old friend or sibling will want to spend the night. Students I spoke with told me this was not a problem and that their roommate was agreeable to working out a schedule. But I heard horror stories from others who told me their roommate had no regard for sleeping or study schedules and just assumed everyone would be "cool" with the situation. Many, it seems, are not.

This is another important matter to discuss before inviting overnight guests. Do not wait until you come back to your room after a day of classes and find a coded note on the door, such as "Do Not Disturb: We're Studying." Yeah, right. As with other matters discussed in this book, respect your roommate's rights and wishes. This is his living space, too, and he is paying just as much as you are to live there.

Guidelines for this vital conversation include:

Are there specific nights of the week you do not want overnight guests?

You may have an early and difficult class on Friday and want to get to bed early the night before. You may have told your roommate last week that you were having a guest over the following Saturday, but she invited someone for the same night after you had made plans.

Is there someone in particular who makes you uncomfortable when he or she visits or stays over?

If a friend or guest of your roommate's has ever acted in a threatening manner or you have felt harassed by that person, you should not tolerate that behavior. As difficult as it may be to tell your roommate this, you have every right to speak out. If your wishes are not respected, tell your RD. There is zero tolerance for threatening behavior or harassment on college campuses.

Is it all right for the guest to use your personal items? Share your food? Use your computer?

The answers can only come from you. Set boundaries and make your wishes known. Do not assume your roommate will know your wishes if you have not shared them with her. (Here is a hint: The answer should be "no." It is not all right for the guest to use any of your personal items. That is why they are "personal.")

What is the arrangement for planning an overnight visit?

You may want to work out a weekly schedule in advance. If your roommate has his girlfriend over every Friday and Saturday night throughout the semester, that is not fair to you. Even if you are not in a relationship, you may still want quiet time on the weekend. If a family member is in town for a few days, work that into the schedule. Again, respect for and cooperation with each other will make the planning go more smoothly.

What is off limits when it comes to overnight guests?

If you are abstinent, do not drink alcohol, or are opposed to drugs, say it now or it will be harder to address later. For example, if you have religious beliefs that promote abstinence, tell your roommate in a manner that is nonthreatening or judgmental. Tell her that you have made a decision to abstain from sexual behavior and that you hope she will respect that. This does not mean she will be abstinent because it is your belief and not hers, but at least you have made your position known.

> **KIM:** A message board near the phone might be a good idea to track phone messages and the schedule of visitors and overnight guests. This way, there are no surprises.

The Third Wheel

When your roommate gets a boyfriend or girlfriend, you suddenly have an additional, and usually unwelcome, roommate. This can cause all kinds of conflicts, from disrupting sleeping and study schedules to jealousy, miscommunication, and problems with university-housing guidelines, which will include a policy on overnight guests. This is also a tricky situation because even though the university has rules regarding overnight guests, you probably do not want to report your roommate to the RD. This will not make you the most popular student on the floor and the tension between the two of you will be close to unbearable. Then what do you do? It gets even trickier when one roommate is abstinent or has strong moral convictions against premarital sex.

I have not even mentioned the problems that come into play when the guest eats your food, uses your clean towels, or sleeps on your bed when you are not there.

If you feel you are always being asked to leave the room to accommodate their private time, stand up for your rights. If you continue to accommodate their requests, your roommate will assume you are all right with the situation when inside, you are fuming. You are paying to live there, too. Even though you do not have the right to tell her who she can have over or whether she can be in a relationship, you do have the shared rights of your living space. Speak directly to your roommate about this and work out a fair agreement. If you go home most weekends, let her know you have no problem with him staying over while you are not there. If you have a good friend down the hall, offer to spend one night a week there. But again, only if you are fine with this arrangement. Do not speak to the boyfriend — this is between roommates and his name is not on the contract.

If the situation is already tense, your roommate may accuse you of being jealous, especially if you do not have a boyfriend at the time. But if you get along with your roommate, and she is respectful of your schedule and asks ahead of time if her friend can stay, and you agree, then all is well. But there is more potential for conflict here than not. Similar conflicts can arise if your roommate has a best friend who spends a great deal of time in your room. Your privacy is affected, as is your quiet study time. If you need to have a conversation with your roommate about the unwelcome boy/ girl/best friend, here are some ways to approach it, depending on the conflict level.

If the situation is tolerable (he is there one night a week), but at some level it is interfering with your schedule or you do not want the situation to escalate:

"I'm really happy for you. Jim seems like a great guy but I wonder if he could stay over Friday or Saturday night instead of Sunday. You know how anxious I get about that early Monday morning lab and how I like to go to bed early."

"Can we alternate weekends so each of us gets a few days to ourselves?"

If the situation is definitely interrupting your schedule (he is there three nights a week) and she leaves notes to "come back later" or asks you to study at the library instead of in your room, it is unreasonable for her to expect that you will accommodate them:

"You know Lisa, I don't mind Jim staying over one night a week, but he's been staying over three nights in a row and it really isn't all right with me. I need some privacy and quiet time during the week. Maybe we could alternate weekends and he could stay over when I visit my folks?"

"Could you spend some time at Jim's instead of him always being here? It's hard for me to study and have privacy when he's in the room so often."

"I don't think it's fair for me to have to stay out of my room because Jim is here. I think you would feel the same way if I constantly asked you the same thing, so we're going to have to work something out."

If the situation is intolerable and his presence is an ongoing disruption to your daily life, explain to your roommate that she needs to either work out a fair arrangement with you, or you will be forced to complain to the RD. She does not want that to happen any more than you do, so there is good chance she will be willing to work something out. Remember, you are both responsible for who you sign into your room, whether it is a friend, family member, or stranger.

Under no circumstances should you tolerate an overnight guest, whether it is a boy/girlfriend, friend, or relative, with whom you are uncomfortable or feel threatened in any way. If this is the case, your well-being is the first priority. Ask your roommate to speak to her in private and be clear with your message. Let her know in no uncertain terms why her guest is not welcome. If she is having different people over on a regular basis, and she is not in a relationship with them, these men are strangers to you (and essentially to her). You should immediately voice your concern to her. Here are some conversation starters:

"Jim has made comments to me that I feel are sexist and it makes me uncomfortable. I do not want him here when I am in the room."

"You know I'm against any kind of drug use, Lisa, so I do not approve of Jim using drugs in our room. If he does it again, I'll go the RD. I don't want to have to do that, but you leave me no choice."

"I'm not comfortable with you bringing strangers to our room. You have just met some of these men and don't know anything about them. What can we do to avoid this again?"

If she ignores your concerns and continues to have strangers over or a man who makes you uncomfortable, go to your RD. Your rights are being violated. Losing a friend is second to any harm that could come to you.

> **KIM:** When someone is in the beginning stages of a romantic relationship, he or she can be oblivious to other people's feelings or to the fact that his or her actions affect someone else.

Sharing is Great, but Not in This Case

Deciding to share belongings is one thing that has been previously covered, but what about sharing information about your roommate? If Marie's mother calls and you tell her she did not come home last night, you are setting up a situation that could result in a panic call to campus security with hysterical parents worried about their child. One student I spoke with, Jamie, told me how his mother called and his roommate told her, "Oh, Jamie is still sleeping. He was out partying all night." It is not your responsibility to report your roommate's comings and goings to his parent unless you think his life is endangered or he is about to hurt himself. In that case, you would call the RD. More on "your responsibilities" in a later chapter. If you have information about your roommate's personal life that is confidential, or better for her sake not to share with anyone else, especially her parents, keep it to yourself. Think how you would feel if your roommate "squealed" on you. You may want to set up an agreeable system for taking phone messages for each other.

How about personal belongings, such as a television? Some roommates think one TV is enough for both of them but this could cause conflicts with viewing schedules. You will have to be flexible when it comes to carving out time for your favorite shows, which may not be her favorite shows. If you both have a favorite show that airs at the same time, take turns each week watching it in the lounge or in a friend's room. Since many students watch shows online or download them to their MP3s, TV sharing is less of an issue than it used to be.

There is room for negotiation when it comes to sharing, and that discussion should take place when you have that first conversation before move-in day. Do not bring two microwaves or two coffeemakers. There will not be room for both of them. As with many other topics covered in this book, communication is the key to a successful roommate relationship. If you make it clear how you feel about sharing personal items ahead of time, you will have taken the first steps to avoiding future conflicts. To provide some guidelines, here is a "discussion" list which includes some items you may not want to share:

- Towels, washcloths, sheets, pillowcases

- Deodorant, hair products

- Combs, brushes

- Clothes

- Toothbrushes, toothpaste

- Make up

- Perfume/cologne

- Jewelry

- MP3s, laptops, desktops, cell phones

Here is a list of items that could be up for negotiation:

- Small appliances allowed under the residence hall guidelines

- Televisions, radios

- Small furniture items

- Bookshelves

- Text books

- Snacks (as long as cost is split)

- Toilet paper, paper towels, tissues (as long as cost is split)

KIM: Do not assume your roommate wants to share her personal items with you. Have a conversation about sharing and if you both agree to it, set up guidelines to avoid future conflict and misunderstandings.

Locking Up

There are several million college students living in dorms across the country, which means there is a high potential for theft. The most commonly stolen items include jewelry, laptops, cell phones, MP3 players, textbooks, and cash. Items can be stolen by someone living in your dorm, a guest your dorm mate has signed in, or your roommate.

Jennifer, a second-semester sophomore I spoke to, told me she repeatedly reminded her roommate, who grew up in a small town, to lock the door, even if she was just going down the hall to the bathroom. When someone stole Jennifer's iPod, after her roommate left the room unlocked while in class, she got into a huge fight with her roommate demanding to be paid back for her loss. (Luckily, her loss was covered under her parents' homeowners insurance.)

It is not only the loss of personal items you should be concerned about, but more important is your and your roommate's personal safety. Just because IDs are required to get into your dorm, it does not mean someone could not be assaulted while in the room alone. You also do not know every guest a dorm mate has signed in. In an ideal world, college students could put complete trust in every other college student, but that is not the world in which we live. Your safety and the safety of your roommates and hall mates should be a number one priority, no matter what the demographic or location of your college. Do not assume a small, private, exclusive college is any safer than a large, urban university. Be mindful of this and protect yourself and your roommates by always locking the door, even to run down the hall to microwave some popcorn. Keep a few keys on university "necklaces" on a hook by the front door. But do not forget to put them back. This way, a key is always available for quick exits and entrances, and it becomes a visible reminder because it is right next to the door. You may want to label the keys with your names as well.

One last word on locking up: Do not, under any circumstances, ever lock your roommate out of her room. If you think it is a joke, it is not funny, and you could endanger that person. If you do it out of spite or revenge, you could (and likely will) have disciplinary action taken against you. If you do it because you have a guest and want some privacy, you have absolutely no right to keep your roommate from entering the room. It is hers as well as yours. She is paying as much as you are to live there.

One student I spoke to told me that someone down the hall locked her roommate out because they had been fighting and she wanted to "get back at her." The locked-out roommate had severe asthma and needed her inhaler. She had to have someone run and get the RD to open the door because she was having trouble breathing. Her roommate thought it was funny until she saw the RD and campus police open the door. Since this was not the first time she locked her roommate out and had endangered her well-being, she was asked to leave the dorm and ended up living off campus.

Here are a few safety tips to keep your room and belongings secure:

- Keep your valuables at home. If you must bring them to your dorm (passport, digital camera, jewelry) hide them. Many thefts happen within a few minutes, when you or your roommate runs down the hall to use the bathroom or microwave and do not lock the door.

- If you make it harder to find valuable items, there is a higher chance the thief will not spend a significant amount of time looking through everything.

- Invest in a laptop security cable. Laptops are one of the most commonly stolen items and unless you carry it everywhere (the bathroom?), it can be stolen in less than a minute.

- This bears repeating: Lock the door. You may feel like you are part of a family in your dorm, but the students are not family members. You may feel as though your dorm mates have a common bond, but that does not mean one of them will not steal from you. Do not be naïve about what can or cannot happen in a college dorm. When you are, your guard is down.

- Keep track of who comes and goes, not only from your room but your floor. If someone suspicious is lurking around or acting strange, call the RA. The same thing goes if you see someone who looks and acts nothing like a college student.

- If your roommate has someone in the room while you are at class, think twice about leaving grandmother's necklace on your bureau. You may get along great with your roommate and her boyfriend, but they are essentially strangers. You have no idea who the people are that he hangs out with and whether there is a possibility they would visit your room while you are not there.

KIM: Even if you think you will be mocked for labeling or locking up your belongings, think first about having to replace your laptop, MP3, or piece of heirloom jewelry (which you should have left at home in the first place).

How to Get Involved

In addition to the benefits of living in an LLC, there are many opportunities for involvement with your university outside your role as a student and roommate. College may be the most culturally rich environment in which you will be involved during your life, a time filled with encouraging new ideas, friendships, and learning experiences. Not only will extracurricular activities benefit your academic and social growth, they will also provide "space" for you away from your dorm room and apart from your roommate. In other words, you do not want to spend every free minute with your roommate, no matter how well you get along.

Extracurricular activities are a good way to get connected to the university and become part of a community outside classes and your dorm. If you are a commuter, part-time, or working student, you will have less time, but there are enough activities even at small colleges from which you can pick and choose. There are schools with hundreds of clubs and, even if you do not find one that matches your interest, you can approach the office of student affairs or housing and ask to start one. Your orientation packet will most likely contain a list of extracurricular activities. You will also find bulletin boards around campus listing events and group activities.

Kelly took up knitting during her sophomore year and found that because of her full class load and part-time work schedule, it was the most convenient activity because she could do it anywhere on campus. She posted a notice in the student activities center, looking for other students who liked to knit. The response was so overwhelming that she ended up organizing a knitting group in five separate dorms. The groups then connected to the office of international students and started a donation drive in which hand-knitted items were sent to children's homes in China.

On-campus jobs are also a good way to meet new people and get involved with another academic area outside your major. When I was an undergraduate at the University of Maryland, I took a work-study position in the music and art library. My first job was to sort and file hundreds of slides of Egyptian pottery that one of the art history professors would use in class. I was a music major and did not know the first thing about Egyptian art. By the end of that year, I could recognize to which dynasty a piece was assigned and interpret some of the markings and glazes. To this day, I remain interested in Egyptian artifacts, pottery, and history.

If you are encountering an ongoing conflict with your roommate, being involved in extracurricular activities will give you the chance to spend time outside your room.

KIM: Finding extracurricular activities that match your interests are not only a good way to get to know the university community but will give you breathing room and time spent separate from your roommate.

4

The Personality Spectrum

If you become a parent, you may spend more time with your child's friends than your own. You will be witness to a spectrum of personality traits, from incessant whining to perpetually runny noses to the constant threat: "I am telling your mom." You will see some of the same traits in college roommates, except the list gets longer and the conflicts more difficult to resolve.

Here is a rundown, from the mouths of actual college students, of the types of personalities you may encounter in a roommate:

The Converter: This person tries to convert his roommate to change diet, religion, political views, or recycling habits. The result will be an annoyed roommate leaving cheeseburger remains, Rush Limbaugh books, and empty soda cans in the room to get the message across that conversion is not an option.

The Natural: This person wears hemp clothing, follows the European approach to hygiene and razors, and has Woodstock posters on the walls. More prevalent in northeastern states, such as Vermont. Less so in Texas.

The Animal: Have you seen the movie "Animal House?" Do you remember the character played by John Belushi? Enough said.

The Geek: There is a reason stereotypes are just that. This is the student who studies every free minute, only socializes with other geeks, and is shunned by other groups of students. However, this is also the personality type that will be driving the Mercedes and showing photos of the beach house at that tenth-year reunion.

The Slacker: This person sleeps through classes, gets high every day, wears shorts and flip-flops in January (in Buffalo), and refers to professors as "dudes."

The Caffeinator: This person cannot go to the bathroom without a cup of coffee. Overly energetic all the time. Sleeps four hours a night. Quickly gets on roommate's nerves.

The Communicator: But not in a good way. This person constantly talks on her cell phone, relating the most mundane events to friends. ("I just took a bite of ramen. What are you doing?") Instant messages and texts during class, meals, and conversations. Sleeps with cell phone under pillow.

The Blender: These are the people you want for roommates. They can adjust to almost any situation. They are good students, good children, well-balanced, and mature but still have fun and take it all in with a grain of salt. After all, it is only college.

KIM: You will encounter a rainbow of personalities in college and throughout your life. Think about how dull it would be if everyone behaved the same and held the same beliefs, ethics, and views. Your experience as a roommate will better prepare you to deal with different personality types in your post-college life.

Every Little Thing She Does Is Not Magic

If anyone reading this book has ended a romantic relationship, you will recall what it is like toward the end, right before the actual breakup. Everything he does annoys you. You can dissect the minutia of every sentence she utters to validate why you are breaking up. The same goes for roommates who may be on opposite ends of the personality spectrum. She spends Saturday mornings cleaning, and you have not seen a rising time before noon on the weekend since sixth grade. Your breakfast menu consists of doughnuts and diet soda, and she brings a tofu omelet back to the room every morning. To annoy you even more, she offers you a bite each time, along with a subtle lecture on improving your eating habits. To annoy her in return, you take a sloppy slug of your 24-ounce diet soda and follow up with a healthy burp.

Remember that some habits can be broken. Throwing dirty clothes on the floor may be a component of someone's personality, but that behavior can be changed through a nonaccusatory conversation. Plus, that behavior affects everyone living in the same space. That behavior clutters an already cramped space. That behavior can cause unpleasant odors in a small space. You get the picture.

However, wanting to wear clean clothes is more of a personality trait than a behavior. It could become a behavior that affects other people if, for example, there was a washing machine in the room and that person used it late at night. You will have to navigate and accept some personality traits that drive you crazy. You cannot expect someone to change entirely to please you any more than you would appreciate him or her asking you to do the same.

The best approach is to talk about it right away. You cannot bring about change by being silently resentful and angry. As you will read later on, use "I" and "you" whenever possible in a non-accusatory, respectful manner, something like this:

"Your gum snapping distracts me when I am studying. You may not be aware that you are even doing it. Could you not snap your gum? I would appreciate it."

"I would appreciate it if you did not leave your nail clippings on the bathroom floor."

The company Nifty Notes has a humorous "Roommate FYI" check-off list you can purchase and post in your room (search for Nifty Notes online for ordering information). Depending on your roommate's sense of humor, some of the check-off items on this list may provide a friendly reminder to her that she shares a space with someone and that someone is you.

Some of the "nifty" check-off tips include:

- Stop whining

- Mind your own business

- Get over it

- Aim for the toilet

- Get out of the relationship

- Clean the toilet

- Ask first

- Pay me back

KIM: Flexibility and acceptance are key to not only a successful roommate relationship, but also any future professional and personal relationship beyond college.

The Neatnik Versus the Slob

Included in the most commonly heard complaint among housing directors, RDs, and college roommates, is about what you consider neat versus your roommate's point of view. This can create a major conflict. If you both live as though you are in the middle of the aftermath of a hurricane, and neither seems to mind, that is great. You have found the perfect roommate. If you both live to organize clothes by color or scrub the toilet, rent out your services within your dorm and become a millionaire before graduation.

It is the in-between, gray area when it comes to cleanliness that creates conflict. Whatever your tolerance for order and cleanliness, you must clean your dorm room. There is really no exception. Dirt creates germs and germs contribute to illness. Dirty clothes smell, as do dirty bodies — but that is covered elsewhere. You will be on the run constantly in college, going from class to class, job to class, or late night to class, and being able to find clean underwear without sifting through a mountain of junk will reduce your stress level.

After college, whether you do your own cleaning or hire someone to do it for you, there will be a schedule. Saturday morning versus Tuesday afternoon while you are at work results in the same thing: a clean living environment. Work out a schedule with your roommate. Type it up, print it out, and post it where it is noticeable. If she does not mind vacuuming, assign her that task every week. If she hates to clean the sink and you do not really mind, take that job. Rotate jobs every other week but do not take it on yourself to run a vacuum at 8:30 on a Sunday morning. That probably will not go over well with your roommate. When you come up with a cleaning schedule, figure out a time and day that works well for the both of you. If someone is expecting family or friends to visit for the weekend, and your cleaning schedule is Monday night, take the initiative and clean before company arrives.

However, all of this is easier said than done. There is a good chance you will be matched with someone whose idea of "clean" does not meet your standards, or the other way around. Being messy can either be a personality trait or a sign of laziness and not caring. Being overly organized can be a sign of obsessive-compulsive disorder and sloppiness can also be a sign of depression — more on these later. Assuming your roommate suffers from neither but just does not care where he tosses his textbooks and smelly sneakers — and you do care — then you have a conflict on your hands.

If you worked out a roommate agreement before moving in, you hopefully included an unofficial "cleaning" or "cleanliness" policy. If either of you lied on your questionnaire about your level of tidiness, one of you is to blame when tension builds. So, let us assume you are faced with this problem: for whatever reason, you, the orderly, neat, love-to-organize-clothes-by-color person are matched with a roommate who considers moving a pile of dirty laundry from one corner of the room to another to be "cleaning." The situation is not intolerable but annoys you. In other words, fungus is not starting to cultivate in the sink, but still, it makes you uncomfortable. You have a few choices.

You can have repeated, calm, and mature conversations with him about respecting each other's space and see if his behavior changes. Let him know this is something that is important to you, but do not go off the deep end with cleanliness standards and cleaning instructions. Just let him know that you are a neat person (as you indicated on your questionnaire) and that you would hope he at least keeps his part of the room and shared space clean.

If you have a great relationship and feel that humor is a good way to approach difficult topics with him, make a joke about how funny it is that you were assigned to live together when you are so opposite. Or, say something like, "Don't expect to borrow my Hello Kitty underwear when you don't have any clean ones left." If that doesn't work, try to gauge the level of slobbery. Is it tolerable? Is it something you can live with? This depends on how it directly affects you. If he is just tossing everything he owns in his closet, but keeping the door closed, there is no reason that you cannot live with this. If he leaves dishes piled up in the sink but does not seem to mind watering the plants and feeding the communal fish, can you come up with a compromise that suits both of you?

The Neatnik Versus The Slob: A Story

Rebecca, a music major who plays the harp, told me how she keeps everything she owns in its place and is fanatical about order and cleanliness, though her behavior does not border on obsessive-compulsive disorder. She said this is because the harp is such a large instrument and, when she was living at home, she had a tiny bedroom. Her parents agreed to buy her a harp if she made room for everything. This encouraged her to come up with some clever strategies to utilize every square inch of her bedroom — the harp literally took up half the room. She was rooming with Jen, who had grown up with four brothers. Jen's house was always a mess and her brothers left their sports gear and dirty sneakers everywhere in the house. Her parents picked up after her brothers but did not set any specific ground rules for them to do it themselves. Her father was a college professor and kept piles of books and papers strewn about the house.

Here is a situation where one roommate was raised in one kind of environment and the other in a different one. The tension over cleanliness between Rebecca and Jen came to a head and they stopped speaking to each other, even though they had a good relationship and enjoyed each other's company. When Rebecca shared the situation with her mother, she told her to assess what was really bothering her. Was it the clutter that Jen kept around her or was it dirt? Her mother pointed out that there was a difference. Rebecca realized that Jen was not an unclean person. She had good hygiene, washed her clothes, and did her share of cleaning. Rebecca discovered it was the clutter that troubled her. Even though she kept her harp in one of the music rooms, she was so accustomed to conserving space that anything out of order, even if it did not belong to her, was annoying. Because they wanted their relationship to work, they sat down and talked about the situation. It was only then that they discovered the different environments in which they were raised. They had a good laugh, shared some harp and brother stories, and came up with a plan that met both of their needs.

KIM: Get acclimated to a cleaning schedule while in college. It will help you transition into apartment dwelling and home ownership. If you studied hard and did well in school, you will be able to afford someone to do it for you. Until then, become friends with the vacuum cleaner.

The Gossip

You have probably heard this from a teacher or parent at some point in your life: no one likes a gossip. Anyone at any stage in life can fall prey to gossip. Gossip is never warranted or deserved. At one time, gossip was only spread by word of mouth, but with unlimited access to the Internet and the speed at which gossip can be spread, there are more dangerous consequences. Young people have committed suicide because of the hurtful rumors and downright lies people can text to friends or post online. One unwarranted rumor started by a student who has a gripe about another can spread like wildfire, and can be impossible to retract or refute.

If you find out your roommate is talking about you behind your back, you can confront her or choose to ignore it. Ignoring it may sound like the more reasonable reaction, but, in reality, it is difficult to do. Your instincts are to fight back and defend yourself. But by confronting your roommate and making it clear you know it was her and that you do not tolerate gossip puts her on the spot. If you do it immediately after finding out, you have a better chance of catching her off guard, as she has not had time to prepare a defense.

The best tactic to stop gossiping in its tracks is to be direct. This is not a time to worry about hurt feelings, especially if you are the person to whom the gossip is directed. Worrying about your popularity or losing friends only prolongs the opportunity for others to gossip about you or a friend of yours. State your position on gossip (you disapprove) to the person you know is doing the gossiping. Avoid name-calling, finger-pointing, and the urge to "get back" by spreading gossip about the person you need to confront. Here are some ways to approach, or not approach, the person who is gossiping about you, a friend, or an innocent stranger:

Accusatory approach: "I know you were talking about me behind my back." This is an open-ended statement in that it gives the other person the perfect opportunity to deny it or act as though he or she has no idea what you are talking about.

Better approach: "Were you talking about me behind my back?" Now the other person has to respond with either "yes," "no," "I have no idea what you're talking about," or "You're crazy/paranoid." If he claims he does not know what you are talking about, there is a good chance he does.

Other approaches (notice the use of "I" and "me," always useful when resolving conflict and making your feelings and position known:

"It hurts my feelings when *I* hear you are talking about me to other people."

"*I* do not tolerate gossip. It is hurtful and demeaning. *I* am sure you would not want people to talk about you behind your back."

"If there is something you want to say about *me*, say it to my face rather than behind my back."

"When you talk about me behind my back, not only is it hurtful, but it is unfair as *I'm* not there to defend myself."

If you choose to ignore gossip and it continues, it may eat away at you, and your resentment toward that person will only grow. However, if you are able to look the other way — good for you. You have risen above the pettiness of gossip.

When it is not gossip, but you have some personal information about your roommate that you know would be hurtful, keep it to yourself. This is not only a good rule of thumb to follow as a college roommate, but in post-college life as well. If you happen to learn information that you feel is either endangering your roommate's well-being or would be emotionally damaging and do not know what to do, think it through before telling anyone. The best bet would be to consult with your school's counseling service or share it with your RD.

The Gossip: A Story

Karen, an undergraduate in her fourth year, found out her roommate Julie's boyfriend was a drug dealer. She knew Julie was a devout Christian who not only abstained from any kind of substance use but openly criticized students who indulged in drugs or alcohol. Karen liked Julie and respected her religious and ethical beliefs but could see she was "blinded" by her feelings for her boyfriend. Karen also knew other students were whispering behind Julie's back, calling her "stupid" for not seeing what her boyfriend was doing. Karen asked the RD what to do and he told her that since Julie's boyfriend came over often, he was endangering both of them by possibly bringing hidden drugs or other drug dealers to their room. Karen took the RD's advice and gently told Julie that there were rumors her boyfriend was a dealer. Julie's initial reaction was to be angry at Karen, accusing her of being jealous and trying to ruin her relationship. But she knew the rumors were true. She just did not want to face the possibility of losing her boyfriend.

Telling the difference between gossip and withholding or sharing personal information is not difficult to differentiate. Gossip is mean, hurtful, and unfounded. Withholding personal information you may have about someone, when their well-being is not in danger, is the smart, mature thing to do, even if you really want to tell someone.

> **KIM:** The tendency for people to gossip does not end in high school. Living in close quarters with other people creates tension that can often lead to gossip. Gossiping is wrong and hurtful to other people. Before you say something harmful about someone else, think about how you would feel if the roles were switched.

The Kleptomaniac

Steal - *intransitive verb:* to take the property of another wrongfully and especially as a habitual or regular practice.

Translation: If someone takes something that does not belong to him or her, that is stealing. If that person has asked ahead of time to use it and indicates he or she will return it that is "borrowing." Big difference.

Some roommates assume it is all right to take something that does not belong to them because you share a room. One student, we will call her Jane, told me how a roommate would always eat her food and then accuse her (Jane) of never buying it. Jane saw the same roommate sleeping with a quilt she knew was missing from a hall mate. It even had the hall mate's name embroidered on it, but the klepto just assumed it was all right for everyone on the floor to share.

If your belongings go missing, someone coming in and out of your room could be the culprit, so be sure you know your facts before accusing your roommate of doing the stealing. The best solution is to set up guidelines when you first move in about using or borrowing personal items. It is easy for some people to confuse the two. Borrowing means you will use something and then give it back, but it should come with a request to do so. A roommate may "borrow" your hair conditioner, use some, and then put the bottle back. If you do not want this to happen, establish guidelines up front.

If he takes your laptop to the library because his does not work, is this considered borrowing or stealing? Does the value of the item play into how you feel about this? To avoid these issues, you may want to think about various situations beforehand. If it is all right to borrow some things and not others, that can be a misleading message. You may want to consider setting a policy of "no borrowing," which means you buy and use your stuff and I will do the same.

But let us say that never happened and your iPod is missing. Here are a few scenarios to help resolve this issue:

Scenario #1: You and your roommate did not draw up guidelines on borrowing or using each other's things. You walk in the room and see your iPod on your roommate's bed. He quickly removes the earphones and places the pillow over the iPod.

"I noticed my iPod is missing. I always keep it in my backpack. Do you know where it is?"

"I don't know what you're talking about."

"I know that is my iPod. Please give it back to me. We should have had a conversation about borrowing each other's personal belongings, but we did not, so let's have one now." (State your position and let him do the same.)

Scenario #2: You and your roommate agreed before moving in that it was not all right to share personal items.

"I know you have my missing iPod. We agreed that it was not all right to share or borrow each other's personal things. I have held up my end of the agreement, and I expect you to do the same, so please do not take anything of mine again."

If the borrowing or stealing continues, tell your roommate you are reporting it to the RD. That may end the behavior, even if you do not tell the RD right away.

KIM: Some people confuse borrowing with stealing. Make your position about both of these issues clear from the beginning of your roommate relationship. If you think your roommate will not understand the difference, set a "no-borrowing" policy.

The Whiner

Here is some advice for when you become a parent: Tell your child he can cry, scream, or rant, but he cannot, under any circumstance, whine. There are few things as annoying as whining because those who do it can never think in terms of solutions. In their world, nothing is right and nothing will ever be right. Every problem, challenge, or situation is unfair. It is not even a matter of having things their way, but rather that they are victims and helpless to bring out the change that will end their whining.

The Whiner: A Story

Joanne and Stacy roomed together during their freshman year. At first, Joanne thought she lucked out getting assigned with Stacy because a few of her old friends from high school were already sharing horror stories about their roommates. Joanne and Stacy had a lot in common and, although they did not have much time to socialize together outside the dorm, they got along well. That is, until the third week or so when Joanne started noticing how Stacy blamed someone or something else for every little thing that did not go her way.

One example is when she felt overwhelmed by homework:

"This isn't fair. I can't do all of this homework. Do the professors expect me to finish all of this? I would have to give up all of my free time to get it done. Even if I gave up my free time, I still would never get it done."

Joanne patiently explained that everyone was overwhelmed with the amount of homework. She suggested that Stacy set aside a certain number of hours every day for homework but also allow for a little free time for a break. That was not a viable solution for Stacy:

"But even if I only take ten minutes to watch TV, I'll still never get it all done."

The amount of time and energy that Stacy invested in whining and complaining could have been devoted to structuring her work and free time. Other things Stacy complained about were having to wait five minutes until a shower became available, the lack of food choices in the cafeteria, the heat, the weather, and how crowded the classes were. The list of potential complaints were endless.

It was not just the complaining that got to Joanne, but the tone of Stacy's voice that started to drive her crazy: that sing-song way of drawing out words that constitutes a whine. Joanne soon realized that nothing would ever be right in Stacy's world. Even though Stacy had the power to take charge of many things she whined about, she was helpless to do so. She did not possess the reasoning skills or energy to resolve what she considered complex situations.

Before the end of the first semester, Joanne confronted Stacy. She told her, "You may not even be aware of this, but you find fault in just about everything and everyone. You never seem happy or satisfied, and I'm at a point where I don't even want to bring anything up with you because you'll find something wrong, no matter what."

Joanne had been reluctant to confront Stacy, but when she replied, "It's not my fault. Nothing is going right. This place is horrible...," Joanne not only knew she had done the right thing but understood it was the end of their roommate relationship. She was prepared to switch rooms or even move back home until another room became available, but Stacy ended up withdrawing from school.

In your post-college life, you will eventually be in a position to weed out the negative people in your life (unless you are related, which becomes more challenging). If a friend complains or whines about everything and anything, it brings negativity into your relationship and, therefore, into your life. If you have a whiner for a colleague, it is a little more difficult to remedy that situation, but you can distance yourself from that person socially. Also, if a colleague is a whiner, other people will be affected as well and there is a better chance that someone else, such as a supervisor, will have to deal with him.

Some people can find fault and negativity in just about any situation. You can try to take control of a conversation with a whiner by asking specific questions or interrupting. Asking him or her to clarify his or her complaint gives the whiner a sense that you are interested in what he or she has to say. You may get to a point in which you have to say, "Well, there does not seem to be any solution that will please you," or, "I don't think any suggestion from me right now will help you solve this problem." It takes effort on your part to try to help a whiner come to a solution or see that there is a way out of what seems to him or her to be a no-win situation.

> **KIM:** People who whine and complain tend to have a negative view of the world. You can try to change their outlook but may end up having to distance yourself or end the relationship.

The Aggressor

The Aggressor: There is a reality TV show called, "The Bad Girls Club," in which a group of self-proclaimed "bad girls" live together in a Los Angeles mansion. There is one girl in particular who fits the perfect description of "the aggressor." When things do not go her way, she acts out and retaliates against anyone she believes has betrayed her. In one episode, she walked down the hall outside the girls' bedrooms and banged two aluminum baking trays together while yelling for everyone to get up. In another episode, she started a hitting match with two girls threw pillows, and then a tantrum. The girls had three reactions: laugh at her behavior and walk away, react in the same manner or try to reason with her. This was not a woman open to discussion and negotiation. She acted and reacted based on her given emotional state. The tray-banging incident escalated and ended up in a physical encounter with the other women until the aggressor was physically subdued.

The Aggressor: A Story

Leslie and Danesha did not get off to a good start the first week they moved into their dorm room. (Leslie tended to be a quiet, laid-back person. People generally, interpreted her as someone who would not do well with confrontation.)

Danesha was the opposite. She liked loud music, talked on her cell phone regardless of where she was or the time of day, and argued with family and friends. Danesha possessed some of the traits of "the whiner," in that she thought nothing ever went her way and that her expectations were never met because someone, or something, was at fault. Over the course of the first few weeks, she accused Leslie of using her hair products, interrupting her while she was talking to a friend on the phone late at night, and even trying to steal her boyfriend. Even though none of these accusations were true, and the last one was outrageous, Danesha would point her finger in Leslie's face, yell at her, and either throw something across the room or slam the door on her way out.

At first, Leslie, so surprised at the outrageous accusations and by Danesha's behavior, would just shrug and leave the room. She realized Danesha had some anger issues. She did not want to confront her and was intimidated by her physical presence. Leslie talked with some friends who advised her to confront Danesha about her aggressive behavior. Here are some the strategies that Leslie could use to challenge Danesha's behavior:

- Wait for the aggressor to stop talking and then ask, "Do you have anything else you want to say?"

- If the aggressor starts up again, be persistent in trying to put a stop to her behavior: "All right. It is good to know how you feel about this, but I wish you would stop yelling."

- If there are other people there, they can gather around you for support.

- Repeat the aggressor's name to try to turn her focus away from what she is saying to you:

  "Danesha…Danesha…Danesha…"

- Reiterate what you think the message they are trying to convey is, combining it with the strategy of saying their name:

  "You're accusing me of using your hair products. That's not true, Danesha."

  "If you can stop for a minute, Danesha, I want to tell you my side of the story."

- If the aggressor interrupts, repeat that you will listen only to what she has to say when she is not yelling or pointing a finger in your face:

  "Danesha, I can only listen to what you want to say if you stop pointing your finger at me."

  "Danesha, if you can stop yelling, I can listen to you."

If her level of aggression increases or you see that you cannot take control of the situation, walk away without saying anything or say, "I'll come back when you're calmer and then we can talk." You do not have to take verbal abuse from your roommate, and if her aggressive behavior continues to a point that it is affecting your living situation, go to your RD or RA.

KIM: While it is intimidating to try to reason with an aggressive personality, often giving him or her an open forum to vent and be heard is what he or she really wants. The individual can be under the impression that no one respects what he or she has to say.

Adjusting Your Attitude

There are aspects of everyone's personality that will annoy another person. If you are rooming with an opposite personality type, whether it is the slob, the whiner, the aggressor, the gossip, the slacker, or the animal, looking for commonalities rather than differences may help reduce tension and conflict. Perhaps you like the same foods or music, or you both shop at the same favorite clothing store. Discovering common ground can open the door to a new facet of your relationship. It can also bring you closer to your roommate and open the door to a conversation about personality differences.

If you try to resolve a conflict with your roommate and he does not immediately respond, try not to take it personally. He may be unaware of any problems or embarrassed and unsure of how to respond, especially if you caught him off guard. Also, the adage that there are two sides to every story is true. Your personality, habits, and behaviors may get on your roommate's nerves. The roles may reverse and you may be confronted abbout your behavior. Take heed of what your roommate has to say. Do not get on the offensive; instead, listen to what he has to say. Do some reflection and see if there is truth to the matter. You can learn about yourself and your perception of other people when you are the one being confronted.

5

Cultural and Social Differences

Before you open your mouth and criticize Catholics, Jews, homosexuals, minorities, liberals, or conservatives, think twice. Do not assume your roommate shares your point of view on anything spiritual, cultural, political, or ethical. Unless you have had a conversation with your roommate about his or her views, be careful what you say, you could easily offend him or her.

Cultures are defined by many things: music, religion, place of birth, politics, clothes, food, and friends. The cultural and social differences that you will encounter depend on where you go to college. You will meet many students from diverse cultural backgrounds throughout your college experience. While most large, urban institutions are the likeliest to house students from many different cultures, smaller, private colleges could be just as diverse. The size of the university matters less than geographic location and degree programs. A Catholic university may have a racially diverse student population, but you will not find many Jews or Muslims there. Even though historically black colleges enroll students of other races, the majority of students will be African-American. At urban universities, or universities with a large number of graduate programs, you are likely to meet international students and students from culturally diverse backgrounds.

While these opportunities offer friendships and experiences one might not gain at a university with a less diverse population, cultural differences can cause unintended tension. Even roommates from the same country who grew up in different regions will have cultural differences. Someone who was raised in an urban area may speak louder and use language that a roommate from a small farming town may find confusing or offensive. The United States is a perfect example of people living in the same country with different accents, cultures, cuisines, religions, values, and beliefs.

KIM: It is not always true that large, urban universities offer the most diverse student populations. Many small, private colleges draw international students because of more focused areas of study.

Overview: Not All Cultures Think, Look, and Sound Alike

If you will be rooming with a foreign student or a student from a different background than yours, that initial conversation (See page 42 "That First Conversation") is a good time to get to know more about his or her culture. This is the time to ask about where he or she grew up, when and why his or her family came to the United States, and what he or she likes or dislikes about living here versus his or her home country. Do not get carried away with too many questions or ask anything of a personal nature because you could mistakenly offend your roommate or it could sound as if you are interviewing him or her. You want to engage him or her in conversation but not overwhelm your roommate, so offer information about yourself and your family as well. Believe it or not, not every culture openly discusses personal experiences like Americans. If your gut tells you she is not ready to answer some questions, hold off until you can get to know her face to face. Also keep in mind that religion or politics are sensitive topics of discussion for some cultures.

Students may come to college with preconceived notions and stereotypes of people from other countries. They may have picked up those from home, school, the area in which they grew up, or through what they have read. Americans may perceive all Asian-Americans as high-academic achievers by nature of their ethnicity. However, academic achievement has more to do with family values, family history, and the pertinent role of education within that culture. There is no better environment than higher education to learn about and dispel stereotypes as you will meet students from worlds and cultures quite different from yours.

What Americans consider acceptable behavior could be taken offensively by other cultures. We (Americans) may not think twice about personal space, touching, eye contact, and attire, but to someone from another culture thses things could be insulting. There are also cultural differences Americans find offensive such as hygiene, woman's clothing, and woman's rights. The perception of privacy is another distinction among cultures. A non-contact culture is one in which close interaction is not the norm. This culture is more sensitive to living with other people in a small place. The divergences listed above, coupled with the language barrier make for an interesting living environment.

Not All Cultures Think, Look and Sound Alike: A Story

Kathryn is a sophomore at Temple University. She roomed last semester with a student from a foreign country. Kathryn told me her roommate only showered once a week and wore heavy perfume. She also mentioned that her roommate's parents visited every weekend. The whole family would come with packed meals and stay for hours. Kathryn would say a polite hello and head to the library or a friend's room. Because Kathryn and her roommate had difficulty communicating due to language barriers, she was hesitant to even raise the issue, fearing she might offend her. She went to her RD who set up an appointment with someone in the office of multicultural affairs. The meeting was helpful as it gave Kathryn some insight into her roommate's culture and suggestions on how to broach the topic with her. When Kathryn did finally bring up the topic of the weekly family visits, her roommate was visibly upset and was unable to express her feelings in English. There was no way Kathryn was going to bring up the hygiene issue after that and started spending more time sleeping at her parents or in a friend's room. She went back to the RD and told him she was willing to move because it was clear that her roommate could not change her cultural behavior overnight, and the tension between them had become too great. The RD met with Kathryn's roommate and her family and found that it was she who wanted to move. She requested to room with a student from the same country as her. It took a month, but the housing office accomodated her. Kathryn was matched with a new roommate, who was American.

This may sound like an extreme example, but it is typical for cultures to clash. If your situation is not as severe and you have minor cultural differences with your roommate that do not require a move, you may, on occasion, say something offensive without knowing. If that happens, apologize to your roommate and tell her:

"I wasn't aware that would be offensive to you. I apologize. I hope you can be patient with me until I get to know you more."

If your roommate is doing something that makes you uncomfortable, like standing closer than you are used to, it is all right to speak up:

"It makes me uncomfortable when you stand close. I'm just not used to it. I don't mean anything hurtful; it's just how I am."

If you simply cannot understand what your roommate is saying, because of a language barrier, be patient. Remember, it is just as difficult for her:

"I'm sorry but I don't understand what you're trying to say." (Offer her a piece of paper)

"Can you draw it for me?" Use English words she has used to let her know you are hearing what she has to say. They can serve as prompts for her and hopefully get her to clarify her thoughts.

KIM: If you room with someone from a different cultural background, it can be a rewarding learning experience for both of you, even if you encounter some barriers.

Language Differences, Bigotry, and Racism

Put simply, do not tolerate language that is politically incorrect or racially divisive, whether it is aimed at you or directly affects you. People of one color think it is all right to make a racially charged remark in front of other people who share their race. However, if you are racist yourself and agree with the remark made by the other person, well, that is too bad for everyone. But before making those comments, look around, especially if you are at a large urban university. There are students of all colors and racial backgrounds and one of them, might end up being your best friend. One of the many great things about the college experience is meeting new people and learning, not only in the classroom, but in your dorm room, the local pub, or the tech center.

If your roommate constantly makes offensive remarks, either about your cultural background or someone else's, let him know immediately:

"You know, when you make those kinds of comments, you are offending not only me but some of my friends. Please don't make them in front of me anymore."

"You are entitled to your opinion, but please don't assume I agree with you because I don't."

"When you say those things, you are not only insulting me but also my family. I'm sure you wouldn't like it if someone insulted your family."

"I don't know where you're getting some of your ideas about my culture, but you're way off base. If you'd really like to know the truth about where I came from and what I believe in, I'd be happy to share it with you."

Language Differences, Bigotry, and Racism: A Story

Marcy was white and roomed with a Jenny, who grew up in a small town in Kansas. Marcy was raised in West Philadelphia, a neighborhood full of cultural diversity. Some of Marcy's best friends from school were African-American. Where Jenny grew up, there were only a handful of African-Americans and she came to college assuming everyone who was white thought the same as she did. Jenny felt it was fine to use hurtful and stereotypical language about African-Americans in front of Marcy, who had never heard that kind of language before. She was appalled that anyone still used those kinds of words but even more appalled that Jenny would think it was all right to do so. At first, she thought her silence would send a message to Jenny. But Jenny did not get the message so Marcy spoke up:

"Just because I'm white doesn't mean I feel the same way as you about people of color. I wasn't raised to make fun of people's differences and I don't want to be around you when you use that language."

Marcy made her feelings known to Jenny. But even if Marcy's outspokenness gets Jenny to think twice about saying these things out loud, there's little chance it will change a way of thinking that Jenny has known her whole life. If Jenny comes from a culture that is not diverse and if she has heard her family and friends make racially charged remarks (and has never lived anyplace else) she is going to carry that "culture" with her to college. This is not to defend Jenny's behavior, but to emphasize that Marcy can try to educate her about diversity and take a stance against hurtful remarks, but Jenny's way of thinking will not be turned around overnight. Turn around over the course of her college stay? Absolutely. That is a possibility but if Marcy feels she cannot live another minute with someone who is a racist, she needs to request a move. Since her roommate has not technically broken any rules, and Marcy's only complaint is her racist attitude, Marcy should be the one to volunteer to switch roommates.

> **KIM:** There are people who cannot be swayed and will never change their views and opinions about a religion or culture different from their own.

I Like Boys. You Do Not

Some straight students have no problem rooming with someone who is openly gay. Others will encounter a gay peer for the first time in their lives, even though they may have known people who had not yet come out. College is when many young people experiment with sexuality, having brief relationships with both men and women, knowing they are straight. It is part of learning, getting to know yourself, and coming to terms with who you are.

So for some students who have gay friends or family members, rooming with a gay student is not a big deal. They can get on your nerves as much as a straight roommate, and you can encounter conflict over issues that have nothing to do with sexual preference. For those who may not be as comfortable in this situation, there are some concerns, questions, and fears that will undoubtedly arise:

- If I'm rooming with a gay student, will people who are just getting to know me think I am gay, too?

- If I start to explain myself, that I am not gay, does this raise a red flag anyway?

- Is there a chance he or she will become attracted to me because we live together?

- I do not want my gay roommate to see me without clothes.

- I have seen homosexual people in movies and TV and I do not want to be associated with them.

- What if my gay roommate has someone spend the night? That will make me twice as uncomfortable.

- I am (religiously/morally) opposed to homosexuality and want no contact with my roommate, who I just found out is gay.

All of these are valid concerns. Just as you may disagree with your roommate's perspective on other issues, such as politics, religion, life style, and friends, you have the right to disagree with his or her sexual preferences. Even if you think you have no problem with homosexuality, living with someone whose preference is the opposite of yours can cause a level of uneasiness not only with you, but with your family and friends.

The best way to "laugh off" accusations from other people that because your roommate is gay, you must be gay, is to do just that: laugh it off. You could just shrug and say something like this:

"Well, for your information, I happen not to be gay."

"That's funny; I wouldn't think you were gay if your roommate was."

The more you try to explain, the more it will appear as if you have something to defend. If you think your parents will be uncomfortable visiting because, for example, your father bad-mouths homosexuals, you should warn your roommate, whom you like and do not want to be embarrassed, and add the caveat that it is your father's viewpoint not yours. You and she may want to make arrangements when she will not be in the room, to avoid a tense situation for everyone. It is not as if your parents are there every weekend (and if they are, you and they should have a talk):

"Look, I just want to give you the heads up that my folks are visiting next weekend and my dad is really opposed to homosexuality. He's not going to change and I accept that about him. I'm afraid he may embarrass you, so are you okay with heading out for about a half hour? They're coming to take me to dinner, so they won't be in the room for long."

If you are the one opposed to homosexuality, it gets a bit more complicated. It is not as if you have someplace else to live. As with any strategy to ward off conflict before it becomes insurmountable, honesty and forthrightness are the best approaches. There are ways to explain your discomfort with or disapproval of your roommate's sexual preference without feelings getting hurt or someone climbing on a political or religious soapbox. Some people disapprove for religious reasons; others think homosexuality is weird or unnatural. It is all right to have these feelings and viewpoints and it is important to share them with your roommate from the start or your resentment will build and communication may break down. Here are some communication strategies and suggested resolutions when homosexuality causes discomfort and uncertainty:

"My religion disapproves of homosexuality. I wanted you to know that. I respect your choices, just as I would expect you to do the same for me."

"I just want you to know that I think homosexuality is unnatural. I'm not comfortable with it, but we have to live together and I hope it won't be a problem for either of us."

"I've never known anyone who was gay. This is all new to me so it's going to take awhile to get used to this situation."

If, at any time while living with a gay roommate, you feel threatened or harassed by him/her or anyone he/she is bringing into your room, tell your RD or RA immediately. The same rules apply regarding harassment whether your roommate is gay or straight. It is always a good idea to become familiar with the university's sexual-harassment policy which is available at the housing office if it was not included in your orientation or admission packet.

KIM: There will be situations in which roommates cannot live together because of opposing life styles and resulting conflicts that cannot be resolved.

Sexual Preference and Conflict

Here is an actual story as told to me by Kylie, a sophomore at a private New England college:

Part way through her freshman year, Kylie's roommate, Janine, came out to her as a lesbian. She had not yet told anyone in her family and was just starting to tell her friends. Janine and Kylie got along but did not spend much time together socializing outside the dorm.

Kylie was a devout Catholic and, like her church, opposed homosexuality. She had never known anyone to come out as gay so this was a new experience for her, and Janine's confession made her immediately uneasy. Kylie decided to be honest about her religious and moral beliefs about homosexuality so she told Janine that she and her church, disapproved. Janine immediately became defensive and told Kylie that there was nothing she (Kylie) could do about it because her life style choice was protected under the university's antidiscrimination policy. The policy only referred to discrimination against a student because of his or her sexual orientation in relation to assigning roommates, so Janine had misinterpreted the language. Even though Janine now knew Kylie's position, she brought her girlfriend to the room several times a week and engaged in sexual activity. Sometimes she would ask Kylie to leave the room and sometimes she would tell Kylie she "didn't have to listen if it made her uneasy." Even though Kylie approached Janine several more times to try to make her understand her position, Janine continued her behavior and the tension between the two became palpable.

Kylie was furious. When Janine's mother called one night, Kylie told her that she was out with her gay girlfriend. When Janine found out, she locked the door from the inside the next night when she knew Kylie had a late class. Kylie couldn't get into her room and repeatedly called Janine on her cell phone, but she did not pick up. Kylie went to the RD who in turn called campus security. Janine received disciplinary action and was moved to another dorm. While awaiting a new roommate, Kylie worried constantly that she would again be matched with a lesbian.

This story contains the worst elements of a bad roommate relationship: betrayal, opposing moral viewpoints, disrespectful behavior, endangering a roommate's safety, and retaliation. What could Kylie and Janine have done differently that would have resulted in a different ending?

Kylie was honest with her feelings about Janine's sexual orientation. She could not have predicted Janine's reaction but that is always a risk when you have to confront someone about an issue on which you both disagree. If Kylie had kept her views to herself, that would not have changed her beliefs or lessened her level of discomfort.

Should Kylie have outed Janine to her mother? No. She was obviously retaliating against Janine without considering the life-altering consequences. Outing a child to his or her parents is cruel and often ends up hurting everyone involved.

Should Janine have been so open about her sexual behavior in the room that was also Kylie's home? Regardless of someone's sexual orientation, openly engaging in that kind of activity is against dorm policies whether it is acknowledged or enforced. Ultimately, Kylie was in a difficult situation. She was morally opposed to her roommate's life style and betrayed her trust while Janine endangered Kylie's well-being and disrespected her rights. When two people are firmly opposed to each other's life style, there is a small chance either will change viewpoints, which can result in an unsolvable conflict. One or both roommates will have to be reassigned if they cannot come to terms with living together and respecting each other's choices.

> **KIM:** Retaliating against your roommate for any reason only results in worsening the tension and heightened conflict.

You Are a What?

You may ask why a section on this topic even needs to be included in this book. It is a relatively new area that is being addressed on campuses across the nation, while it has yet to be heard of at others. However, as with much of this book, the information in this section is designed to prepare you for circumstances you may encounter as a college resident.

A "trans" or "gender-nonconforming student" are terms you should become familiar with, as they are receiving more national and media attention as more students go public with their stories.

A trans student is someone who has decided to live life, including that at college, as a member of the opposite gender. A transmale is a woman who lives her life as a male, but is still technically a woman. He may have a girlfriend, receive testosterone shots, have corrective surgery, and legally change his name, but he chooses to attend a women's college, as they are often places that foster progressive thinking when it comes to gender roles. And women's colleges would be considered a safer environment for the trans student for several reasons: There is no additional physical threat to students, and the trans student has more in common with women students. Colleges at which trans students have a presence have created transgender or gender-neutral bathrooms, changing rooms, and locker rooms. Terminology to raise awareness of this student population includes:

- transgender

- transmale(s) or transmen

- trans person

- trans people

- trans activist

- trans organization

- trans identity

- trans college students

- trans community

You may be scratching your head, trying to figure out what this has to do with you. Well, let us say you are a female student and are assigned to a trans-student roommate — someone who was born as a female but lives life as male. The question is whether you are rooming with a male or female student. A feature story in *The New York Times Magazine* stated that "147 colleges and universities nationwide include 'gender identity and expression' in their nondiscrimination policies." The article included one example of a transboy student who enrolled at a private women's college. His roommates complained to the RA about being asked to share a room with a man. The student told his roommates on the first day that he was a "transboy." However, the women were troubled by this on several levels: They were attending a women's college to learn and live in a single-gender environment, and they felt uncomfortable referring to him by male pronouns, since in their eyes, he was still a women. This person ended up transferring to another college, and other students in this situation find themselves isolated, unless their university has a trans organization in which they can become involved and meet students with similar issues.

Since most universities state that housing assignments cannot be based on sex or gender, you might not know until your roommate announced as such that you were assigned to a trans student. If this is the case and it makes you uncomfortable, you should take it up with your RD immediately. The most likely outcome is that student will be reassigned or will receive help from the housing office to relocate.

> **KIM:** Throughout your college years, you will encounter students who have chosen nontraditional life styles. Part of a college experience is to meet new people, make new friends, and learn about life choices that are different from your own.

Raising Awareness

College is a place to explore new ideas, forge new friendships, and discover cultures, communities, and ideologies that make up a well-rounded education. You will have the opportunity to interact with people from walks of life similar and quite different from yours. Some universities will offer more multicultural organizations and clubs than others. Religious schools and schools with targeted academic areas of study, such as the music conservatory I attended as an undergraduate, may offer fewer because of size, smaller enrollments, and narrow mission statements.

If you are looking for a diverse campus, the "*U.S. News and World Report's America's Best Colleges*" is a good place to start, with its lists and profiles of those universities and colleges. For example, if you are gay, you would likely want to steer away from religious schools and instead look for those that have previously established clubs and support groups for gay, lesbian, bisexual, and transgender students.

If a cross-cultural curriculum is important to you, look for schools that offer coursework in global issues, gender roles, world religions, social activism, and programs abroad. Those are also the schools that are more likely to offer extracurricular opportunities and organizations that mirror those academic areas.

6

When There is a Serious Problem

Reah's roommate, Pam, seemed moody all the time. She cried often, did not shower for days, and would sleep through classes. When the weather got warm, Rhea noticed that Pam always wore long sleeves. She did not think much about it until she walked in on Pam getting changed one morning and saw small, red lines on her arms.

Rhea remembered a pamphlet she received from student-health services on depression. She looked through it and concluded that Pam may be cutting herself in addition to suffering from depression. Some of the key symptoms were evident: marks on her arms, covering up her arms, sleeping a great deal, crying, and not attending to personal hygiene.

Rhea and Pam got along as roommates, but did not socialize outside the dorm room, so Rhea was not even sure who her friends were or what her family situation was. Rhea was sympathetic to Pam's situation and asked her mom for advice. Her mother suggested she contact the counseling center to find out how best to approach Pam or whether to approach her at all. While she was apprehensive of the fall-out should she confront Pam, she felt obligated to confront her in a gentle way. The counseling center was helpful and suggested that rather than verbally raise the issue, which could lead to an argument or make Pam feel as though she were being attacked, that Rhea write her a letter. She did that, expressing her concern that Pam was sad and unhappy and offering to help her get counseling.

After a few days, Pam left a note for Rhea, telling her she felt lost and overwhelmed at school and was afraid to tell her parents. Rhea and Pam finally talked and Rhea accompanied her to her first counseling session on campus. Although Pam never came out and asked for help, her actions were, essentially, a cry for help and she was fortunate to have a roommate who cared.

Was Rhea obligated to help Pam? No. Pam was responsible for her own actions, as she was responsible for making the decision to seek, or not seek, treatment. If Rhea had witnessed Pam in a situation of immediate danger, she would be morally obligated to take action, but reaching out to a roommate in emotional distress is not a requirement to living in a dorm. Some roommates may want to look the other way and not get involved. If you do want to offer help, only a mental-health professional can make a diagnosis.

Substance Abuse

College is a pivotal point in an 18-year-old's life, a time in which he or she is most likely experiencing the first extended period away from home and newly found independence. Even if you are enrolled at a college that is considered safe and inclusive, drug, alcohol, and tobacco use will be an issue for some students. Students may view colleges as a hotbed of opportunity to experiment and freely abuse prescribed and illegal substances.

Note: Students 21 years or older are allowed to possess/consume alcohol in rooms and anywhere else on campus, but there are applicable restrictions stated on the university's policy on drugs and alcohol.

Drug and alcohol abuse are not just a problem for the students who are abusers, but for parents, teachers, friends, and more. Students living on campus are directly affected by drug use and its consequences. Statistics can be skewed and should be interpreted carefully. In 2007, USA Today cited a study that reports "nearly half of America's 5.4 million full-time college students abuse drugs or drink alcohol on binges at least once a month," calling this an "urgent problem on campuses across the nation." The study also cites that "alcohol is the favored substance of abuse on college campuses, but the abuse of prescription drugs and marijuana has increased dramatically since the mid 1990s."

Colleges promote a learning and living environment that is free of drug and alcohol abuse and prohibit the unlawful manufacture, distribution, possession/use of alcohol, illegal drugs, or controlled substances on their property. Federal and state laws prohibit the possession, sale, and consumption of alcohol by minors, anyone under the age of 21. Disciplinary action, including suspension or dismissal and arrests may result for anyone engaged in these actions. Immediate removal from your dorm may also be a consequence, depending on housing policies. The local police department will be contacted when drugs or drug-paraphernalia are found on campus. This could result in a monetary fine and imprisonment. In sum, abusing drugs or alcohol is a serious offense on college campuses.

Many students use prescribed stimulants obtained from other students to help them pull an all-nighter, unaware of the inherent dangers in using medications that have not been prescribed to them. Illegal drugs can be even more dangerous, resulting in permanent damage to someone's health and pssible death. Inhalants are one type of drug that can cause long-term and severe side effects, such as suffocation, nosebleeds, and loss of sense of smell. They can also result in liver, lung, kidney, and brain damage. Crack cocaine is another illegal drug that can be combined with other types of drugs. Ingesting crack, which has a number of street names, including "snow" and "blow," can result in heart attack, seizure, or respiratory failure.

Abusing illegal drugs can lead to a potential and fatal overdose. Because they are not manufactured under controlled conditions one does not know their composition. It is also not possible to know the strength of these drugs and students may unintentionally mix a fatal combination of illegal substances with alcohol that can cause serious injury or death.

Alcohol is the most common substance abused by college students, partially because it does not have the same dangerous reputation as, say, cocaine or "ecstasy." Furthermore, alcohol consumption is viewed as a way of life on campuses around the country. The side effects of ongoing alcohol use can lead to long-term health problems, low grades, personality changes, and possible expulsion from the dorm or university. Alcohol poisoning is a series of physiological reactions to alcohol and toxic by-products. Signs that someone has ingested toxic amounts of alcohol include mental confusion, coma, inability to be roused, slow or irregular breathing, vomiting, and hypothermia. Someone can still have alcohol poisoning without showing these symptoms. Untreated, the effects of alcohol poisoning can lead to permanent brain damage or death.

Alcohol use also lowers a person's inhibitions, leading college students to act in ways that are not only inappropriate or risky, (driving when intoxicated or jumping off buildings) but unlike anything they would do when sober. Women should especially be cautious of date rape, or being intoxicated can impair their judgment and that of those around them.

KIM: You have the right to tell your roommate if her excessive drinking or drug use threatens your safety or compromises your status as a dorm resident.

Substance Abuse and Your Roommate: What You Can Do

What action should you take if your roommate is abusing drugs or alcohol? First, assess whether your safety is being compromised. As a dorm resident, you may be held accountable for illegal activity taking place in your room, whether or not you have initiated it. If there is any kind of illegal drug activity taking place in your dorm room, be adamant with your roommate that you will not tolerate it and that you will report him or her to the RD if it happens again. If you need other advice, go to the counseling or student-health center. Sessions are confidential so your name will not be attached to your inquiry. Let the counselor know you want your roommate to get help.

Do not cover for your roommate or enable him to skip class, miss work, or lie to family and friends. It is likely he will deny he has a problem, and will instead try to convince you it is only a weekend activity or that he can stop at any time. Use the same approach tactics as you would for a roommate with depression or an eating disorder: be sensitive but firm in your position. If there was a particular incident or a repeated behavior that frightened you or compromised your daily life, be honest. As always, encourage him to seek professional help:

"I cannot take any more of you coming in at 3 a.m. and getting sick in the bathroom. It is not fair to me and I think you need to get help."

"I found a needle in the bathroom trash. I want to give you a chance to tell me what's going on before I go to someone about this. Doing drugs in our room is unacceptable to me."

"I was really scared the other night when you brought your friends home so late. You were all drunk and I had to spend the night in a friend's room. This can't happen again."

If you are ever faced with the possibility that your roommate is suffering from a drug overdose, the signs to look for include: slurred speech, obvious lack of coordination, abnormal breathing, slow or rapid pulse, big or small pupils, heavy sweating, hallucinations, and unconsciousness.

Do not be afraid to call for help. You may be worried that you will get your friend in trouble or, if you have been using, you will be in trouble, too. But by not doing something there is a real threat, this person could be permanently impaired or even die. Call campus security or 911 for an ambulance. Another good number to have around is the Poison Control Center at 1-800-222-1222. You will be automatically connected to the center nearest you. Better safe than sorry.

KIM: If your roommate has overdosed on drugs or is intoxicated and suddenly becomes hostile or violent, your safety is a priority. Call the police, then go to another room and lock the door until help comes.

College Students and Mental-Health Issues

We often hear that college represents some of the best years of our lives. While college provides an ideal setting for intellectual and personal growth, it can be overwhelming for the average student and even more so for those with existing mental-health issues.

The causes of mental illness in college students may result from unresolved childhood issues, the stress of adjusting to a new life away from home, making the transition from childhood to adulthood, ending or beginning a romantic relationship, family issues, or having difficulty coming to terms with national tragedies (September 11 or Virginia Tech shootings, for example). The most common mental-health issues experienced by college students in the 21st century include:

- Depression

- Anxiety disorders

- Self injury

- Eating disorders

According to college counseling centers, more students are arriving on campus with a range of mental-health problems and high stress levels. Some college counseling centers are struggling with higher demands of students seeking services. A 2006 survey completed by the International Association of Counseling Services states that "92 percent of college counseling directors believe the number of students with severe psychological problems has increased in recent years."

Colleges and universities are redoubling their efforts to address the increased demand on services by hiring additional counselors to cut appointment wait times. To reduce the stigma associated with seeking counseling, more universities and colleges are implementing outreach, peer-to-peer groups, and providing training sessions for all students on how to recognize signs of mental illness. Many are also offering free counseling sessions or ensuring that visits are covered under the university's student health-insurance program.

Prospective students with existing mental-health issues that will require ongoing treatment, should, along with their parents, investigate the university's services before they enroll. Check the Web site to find out the fee schedule and the number of counselors on the staff. If a learning disability is involved, it is a good idea to find out what kind of special services are offered as well.

Recognizing the Symptoms

If you suspect your roommate is showing signs of mental

illness, you are not obligated, but advised to share your concerns without judgments or accusations. If you see a person who is clearly suffering emotionally, approach him or her with empathy and understanding. You want to avoid embarrassing your roommate or putting him or her on the defensive. A suggested approach would be:

"I noticed you have been acting differently and I'm concerned. Is there anything I can do to help?"

"I'm concerned about you and I'm not sure what to do. I'm here to help if you want to talk about it."

"I know you do not want to talk about this right now, but I picked up some information. I'll just leave it here for whenever you want to look at it."

"If you want to go to the counseling center, I'll help you make the appointment and even go with you if you'd like."

Know that nothing you say, unfortunately, can make him or her automatically feel better or make problems disappear. But taking the first step and offering to help may be the turning point that gets him or her the professional help he or she needs.

Before you approach your roommate, you may want to become educated on the university's counseling center: where it is located; if there is a waiting list for appointments; and what the fee schedule is. This information will better prepare you to offer assistance, especially if your roommate is unable to do this on her own. If your roommate has health insurance, he or she can find out if the university's services are covered under his or her plan. In every case, you want to assure your roommate that help is readily available and services are confidential.

If you suspect your roommate is at risk to herself or someone else, you should call for emergency help if there has been a suicide attempt, an obvious suicide threat, or other behavior that warrants action. If your roommate is acting erratically and you feel threatened or endangered in any way, call your RD or RA immediately. If the situation has escalated to the point where you cannot wait for the RD or RA (it is rare that someone on the housing staff is not in the dorm to help), call campus security or 911.

Depression

KIM: If you are serious about trying to help your roommate suffering from a form of mental illness, first educate yourself to recognize the symptoms. Seek help through the university's counseling or student health offices. Do not try to help when uninformed.

Symptoms of depression include: sadness and anxiety; decreased energy or fatigue; loss of interest or pleasure in usual activities; sleep disturbances; appetite and weight changes; feelings of hopelessness, guilt, and worthlessness; thoughts of death or suicide and suicide attempts; difficulty concentrating, making decisions, or remembering; irritability or excessive crying; and chronic aches and pains not explained by another physical condition. Stressful events or major life-style changes such as divorce, death of a loved one, serious illness, can trigger episodes of depression.

In addition to the resources students can find within the university's counseling and student-health centers, many are educating housing staff on recognizing the signs of depression to help guide students toward treatment. You can express your concern by gently stating, "I don't mean to upset you or make you angry, but I hate to see you like this. How can I help?" Another approach is to say, "I'm concerned about you, your health and your safety. I'm here to help."

Signs of bipolar disorder including alternating feelings of depression and mania, recognizable by increased energy, an unrealistic sense of accomplishment or power, a rapid flow of ideas, spending sprees, and making unplanned and poor business or life decisions.

The Depressed Roommate: What You Can Do

People suffering from depression have little or no desire to engage in the activities they are used to doing. Hobbies they may have had and loved for years no longer hold any interest for them. For some, to even get out of bed, shower, and get dressed is an overwhelming thought. Even if they are around other people — people they may know and care for, they have little to no desire to interact — they feel isolated and alone.

The National Mental Health Association Web site (**www.nmha. org**) offers comprehensive information about the signs of depression and coping skills for college students either suffering from the illness or living with someone who is:

- Get to know where the counseling-services center is on campus. Be sure updated medical records, including medications, are on file.

- Plan your day and set aside time to organize your workload.

- Plan your work and sleep schedules so important class work is not left until the end of the day. Being overly fatigued can be a trigger for depression.

- Participate in an extracurricular activity that brings about opportunities to meet people with shared interests.

- Seek support from other people, such as a roommate, friend, or family member. Sharing your feelings reduces isolation.

- Try relaxation methods, such as meditation, deep breathing, warm baths, long walks, and exercise.

- Take time for yourself every day, even if it is only for 15 minutes a day.

- Work toward recovery by seeking and continuing treatment.

KIM: Do not play doctor or therapist to the roommate who suffers from depression. Instead, listen and offer to help or assist her in seeking help.

Suicidal Thoughts or Actions

According to the Suicide Prevention Network, suicide is the

third-leading cause of death for those between the ages of ten and 24 and the second-leading cause of death for American college students (Kochanek, Murphy, Anderson, and Scott). According to a 2006 American College Health Association report, more than 40 percent of college students have felt so depressed they could not function. The tragic shootings at Virginia Tech in 2007 have highlighted even more the undetected and untreated issues of mental health.

If you suspect your roommate may be having suicidal thoughts, here are some warning signs to help you determine if his or her life is in danger. If your roommate:

- Talks about death, dying, or any specific way she or he may die, such as gunshot, hanging, overdose, jumping, or other methods

- Has suffered or experienced a recent loss — death of family member or close friend, divorce of parents, terminal illness of someone close to him or her, job, financial security, religious faith, or interest in activities

- Shows signs of depression

- Displays a noticeable change in personality: normally cheerful to sad and withdrawn; normally calm to irritable and nervous; normally organized to indecisive and sloppy; or sudden mood changes from sad to happy and energetic

- Displays different sleep patterns — waking earlier than usual, sleeping more than usual, or unable to sleep

- Displays different eating habits — loss of appetite or

increased appetite

- Talks about feeling worthless, helpless, guilty, useless, not having self-esteem, not being of any use to anyone, that there is no hope for the future, or saying something similar to, "Things would be better without me"

If you suspect your roommate may be planning to harm himself or herself or may try to commit suicide, or if you are thinking of hurting yourself, call the National Suicide Prevention Lifeline at 1-800-273-TALK (8255) or the National Hopeline Network at 1-800-SUICIDE (784-2433).

Be especially concerned if you know this person has attempted suicide in the past. According to the American Foundation for Suicide Prevention, between 20-50 percent of people who commit suicide have had a previous attempt.

Take the threat seriously if your roommate or someone else you know shows signs of depression and is contemplating or talking about suicide. Ask if he or she has a plan, weapon, or pills. Ask if he or she has taken any pills. Do not try to talk him or her out of it. Instead, let him or her know you care and are there to listen. Avoid saying, "But you have so much to live for," or "Everything will be fine."

Help the individual seek help, even if he or she does not think it is needed. You may have to show persistence. If he or she is unable to, offer to call a suicide hot line or call campus security or the university's suicide-crisis hot line if applicable. If your roommate has already harmed himself or herself, call 911 and then notify the front desk immediately.

Do not leave him or her alone. If you have to leave before help arrives or she or he gets immediate help, have someone else stay. If he or she appears drugged or incomprehensible, call 911 and notify the front desk immediately.

Listen to what he or she is saying. Take the initiative to ask him or her what he or she is planning but do not attempt to argue or convince him or her there is an alternative. Rather, let the person know that you care and understand and are listening. This is not the time to judge or criticize.

Remove any weapons or drugs that may be used. Accompany him or her to the nearest emergency room if there is no one else there. It is all right to contact the RD so you have additional support. The RD will make the decision to contact parents.

Continue to support your friend. Encourage him or her to continue therapy and take medications.

> **KIM:** If your roommate expresses suicidal thoughts or actions, do not dismiss him or her. If she or he cannot seek help on his or her own, intervene on his or her behalf. Better safe than sorry.

Eating Disorders

Eating disorders affect people of all ages but are especially prominent in college students. According to the National Eating Disorders Association, 2006 statistics show that 20 percent of college students either believe they may have or have been diagnosed with an eating disorder.

This is a serious health concern that can result in chronic health problems and even death. Young people who suffer from eating disorders have creative ways of concealing them and are in denial and refuse to seek treatment. It is possible for a roommate to hide an eating disorder from you, especially if you do not take meals together. You cannot solve or take responsibility for an eating disorder that belongs to someone else.

Eating disorders are not caused by any one thing but result from a combination of emotional, biological, interpersonal, and social factors. It is also likely that these disorders are a manifestation of a desperate need to establish some control and are triggered by stress. The transition to college, pressure to get good grades, and adjustment of living independently are stressful enough for students without eating disorders and can be triggers for those with them. The infamous "freshman 15," which represents weight gain upon entering college, only adds to the pressure for college students to lose weight.

Eating Disorders and Your Roommate: What You Can Do

A roommate with an eating disorder not only disrupts your life and studies but can draw you into her obsession with food and body-image issues. Eating disorders are not actually about food; this kind of behavior is an attempt to gain control over body image and the pressure to comply with societal norms. While you cannot solve or take responsibility for her problems, you can become educated, aware, and offer help if you find yourself living with a roommate suffering from anorexia or bulimia. Here are some warning signs to look for:

Anorexia nervosa - self starvation and extreme weight loss

- not eating or eating small quantities of food and weighing portions beforehand

- fixation/obsession with food or rituals developed for preparing and eating food

- constantly weighing one's self

- distorted body image

- wearing baggy clothes to hide weight loss

- social withdrawal

- excessive exercise

- depression

- fear of gaining weight

Physical signs of anorexia include dry, flaky skin, thinning hair, and cracked or broken nails. Women with anorexia stop menstruating.

Bulimia nervosa, or "Bulimia" — cycle of binge eating and self-induced elimination of food

- eating large amounts of food in a short time followed by self-induced vomiting

- misuse of laxatives, enemas, diuretics, or other medications

- fasting

- eating in secret

- hiding food

- out-of-control eating

- noticeable feelings of loneliness and inadequacy

- distorted body image

Physical signs may include discolored teeth, bad breath, swollen glands, staining or deterioration of tooth enamel, broken blood vessels around the eyes, fatigue, and stomach pain. Women with bulimia stop menstruating.

Binge-eating disorder — uncontrollable, excessive eating followed by feelings of shame and guilt. Those with binge-eating disorder do not purge their food. However, many who have bulimia also have binge-eating disorder and are overweight or obese. They feel as if they have no control over their behavior and feel shame and remorse after eating.

Some signs of binge-eating disorder include:

- eating in secret

- hiding food

- eating when stressed or overwhelmed

- inability to control amount of food

- constantly trying different diets

If you do not deem the situation to be an emergency (if your roommate or friend is not passing out, losing a significant amount of weight, or exhibiting signs of depression or self-harm), you can approach your roommate directly or seek assistance from university counseling on how to sensitively broach the topic. You can also educate yourself on eating disorders through pamphlets or seminars offered through student health or the counseling center.

If you directly address the issue with your roommate, pick a time when no one else is around and there will be no interruptions. Avoid making comments about her body or appearance. Do not "police" her food intake. People with eating disorders have a skewed body image and complex relationship with food.

Start with some positive attributes about your roommate, then focus on your concern, and state the behavior you have noticed that initially raised concern. State the outcome you would like to see. Use "I" statements when appropriate. Do not be disappointed if the first conversation does not go as planned. You may have to start the same conversation more than once so that she hears your ongoing message of concern and offer to help. An example is:

Positive comment:

"You and I get along so well. I'm lucky to have you as a roommate."

State your concern:

"I'm concerned about the amount of weight you've lost the past few weeks."

"I'm worried about how sick you are."

Noticeable behavior:

"I've noticed you take your meals back to the room. We miss you at our table."

Desired outcome:

"I'd like to help you get treatment."

"I'll be happy to find out what kind of counseling is available for you."

"The university has a support group and crisis hot line. I have the number here for you to call."

You cannot or do not want to try to take control of behavior. You also do not want to tell her "things will get better," or to "snap out of it." Both are unrealistic. If either of you become upset or defensive during your conversation, it will only set things back for her. Take a break and suggest you talk later:

"I think we need a break. Would you like to take a walk and talk about something else?"

"Maybe we can talk about this tomorrow. I didn't mean to upset you. I just want to help in any way I can."

Eating Disorders and Your Roommate: A Story

Ashley roomed with Veronica for a full semester before noticing signs of an eating disorder. Veronica was not on the meal plan so Ashley never saw her in the cafeteria. She did, though, wonder how Veronica got her meals and where she ate them. She realized she never saw Veronica eat but noticed she drank a great deal of coffee and energy drinks. Because she was overwhelmed with a full class load and a part-time job, it was not until the second semester that Ashley noticed how much weight Veronica had lost. She saw her coming out of the shower one morning and was shocked at the way Veronica's bones stuck out at her shoulders and hips. Because they both got along well and Ashley knew Veronica's parents had gone through a recent and angry divorce, she wanted to help. She went to the campus counseling center and got a brochure on anorexia. She also talked to a counselor to find out how she might bring up the topic.

She gently began the discussion by reminding Veronica what a good roommate she was and said that her parents were divorced as well. Sharing this common bond was a good approach to broaching a difficult topic and led to Ashley's admission that she noticed how thin Veronica was getting and offered to help. At first Veronica became defensive and denied any issues with food; so Ashley backed off and went to class but assured her she would be open to talking about it further later in the day. That night, Ashley was going to a movie at the student center and invited Veronica, something she had not done before. It took some coaxing, but Veronica went and along the way, admitted to Ashley that she could use someone to talk to and that she was feeling overwhelmed with issues at home and adjusting to college. The next day, Ashley gave her number to the university's eating disorder hot line and sat with Veronica while she made the call. She also accompanied her to the first visit and agreed not to tell anyone, including Veronica's parents, as long as she continued to seek treatment.

> **KIM:** You are not responsible for your roommate's eating disorder and cannot make it go away. While you want to be empathetic, do not let her issue become part of your life and infringe upon your daily routine or social activities.

Self-Injury

A 2006 study conducted by Cornell and Princeton researchers cites "about 17 percent of college students — 20 percent of women and 14 percent of men — report that they have cut, burned, carved, or harmed themselves in other ways. However, fewer than 7 percent of the students studied had ever sought medical help for their self-inflicted physical injuries."

According to the same study, "Self-injury or self-harm is defined as inflicting harm and pain to one's body without intending to commit suicide; the person who self-inflicts does so to cope with emotional pain or traumatic events."

A 2006 Internet study published by WebMD Medical News indicates that students with a history of self-injury are more likely to be women, bisexual, or those questioning their sexual orientation. Repeated self-injury is also linked to psychological distress, eating disorders, and a history of physical, sexual, or emotional abuse.

The warning signs of self-injury include:

- Compulsion to injure oneself by burning, cutting, hitting, scratching or pulling hair or skin

- Scarring on wrists, arms, abdomen, legs, head, or chest

- Hiding arms or other body parts where injury is noticeable

- Hoarding sharp objects, such as razor blades

- Feelings of euphoria during infliction

- Recurring thoughts of self-injury

Living with someone who is a self-injurer can be disturbing, frightening, and disruptive of your studies and daily life. You are not responsible for your roommate's behavior and cannot cure her desire to self-injure. Removing dangerous objects or telling her to "snap out of it," will only deepen her feelings of inadequacy. As when dealing with a depressed roommate, offer your support and lend a sympathetic ear. Offer to find out what resources are available on campus so she can get help. Even though most people consider this behavior bizarre and unimaginable, it is a real and a desperate way of coping for those who live in that world, so do not be judgmental or critical.

As with any mental-health issues your roommate exhibits that affects your routine and ability to study and feel safe in your dorm room, you do not have to carry the burden of knowledge on your own. If your roommate consistently denies there is a problem or refuses to seek help and the situation is worsening, seek the advice of the RD, RA, counselor, or a professor. The counseling or health-services staff is well versed in substance abuse and denial and will be able to offer you guidelines on how to handle the situation. Take this route before considering calling your roommate's parents. Think how you would feel if your roommate did the same to you. Calling her parents only puts you in a compromising position with them and your roommate.

KIM: If your roommate is depressed, suicidal or showing signs of self-injury, do not be judgmental or condescending as it will worsen the situation and further isolate her.

Anxiety Disorder

According to the National Mental Health Association, "College students are becoming the newest face of anxiety disorders," but only half of all Americans struggling with the condition seek treatment.

Every adult experiences various levels of stress at one time or another. It is a part of daily life and helps us solve problems and get through challenging situations. Levels of stress can be heightened at college where finals, new relationships, peer pressure, career choices, the availability of alcohol and drugs, and adjusting to independent living can trigger anxiety. Those individuals who suffer from anxiety-related disorders believe they can control them so they may go untreated.

The most common types of anxiety disorders are:

- Generalized anxiety disorder

- Panic disorder

- Obsessive-compulsive disorder

- Social-anxiety disorder

- Post-traumatic stress disorder

Generalized anxiety disorder (GAD) is defined as having unrealistic, excessive worries about everyday things, expecting the worse and feeling powerless to control these feelings. Symptoms may include irritability, difficulty sleeping or fatigue, difficulty concentrating, and muscle tension. Some of these symptoms can occur daily. For college students suffering from GAD, there is much to worry about: grades, making new friends, safety, homesickness, and pressure to assimilate.

Panic disorder is defined by recurrent and unexpected panic attacks. Symptoms of a panic attack may include heart palpitations, chest pain, a smothering feeling or need to escape, a disconnect from surroundings, sweating, trembling, and fear of dying or losing control. For college students suffering from panic disorders, moving about on a crowded campus, living in a cramped dorm room, or feeling stressed over exams or finals can trigger the symptoms. If your roommate is experiencing a panic attack, try to get her to breathe slowly and deeply as quick breathing only exacerbates the problem. See if you can get her away from the situation that may have brought on the attack; take her on a walk or to some place to get her mind off what is happening. Never suggest that she drink alcohol or take a tranquilizer as they can have an opposite effect and make the situation even worse.

Obsessive-compulsive disorder (OCD) is defined by obsessive thoughts and actions that can control and disrupt a person's daily life and ability to form friendships and relationships. Symptoms may include complex, ritualistic behaviors and routines, such as repeated checking, counting, hand washing, and overall feelings of worry. People suffering from OCD may realize their behavior is out of the ordinary but are unable to control it. Living with a roommate with OCD can be frustrating and difficult to understand for the other person and may impede on his or her comfort level in the dorm room. Most people experiencing OCD will need specialized therapy and perhaps controlled medication to overcome the disorder as it is not likely to disappear on its own.

Social anxiety disorder (SAD) prevents the development of relationships and participation in social and professional activities in which other people are involved, such as parties, public speaking, and meetings. Symptoms may include heart palpitations, blushing, trembling, stammering and light-headedness. For college students who suffer from SAD, being called on in class or being in a social situation in which they do not know anyone, can trigger the symptoms. As in OCD, there is specialized therapy available for those who suffer from SAD.

Post-traumatic stress disorder (PTSD) affects people who may have experienced or witnessed a traumatic event, such as a serious accident, natural disaster, war, the sudden death of a loved one, or a violent personal assault. Most people eventually recover from these types of trauma, but for those with PTSD, depression, anxiety disorders, and withdrawal from family, friends and society are some things that need to be dealt with. College students who are victims of rape or physical assault are candidates for PTSD.

A combination of cognitive-behavioral therapy and medications are commonly used to treat anxiety disorders. If you are living with a roommate who suffers from one or more of these disorders, it will be frustrating and may affect your interaction with her and, possibly, your daily life. College is a stressful time, so you do not want to jump to conclusions if your roommate talks about feeling stressed or displays some associated behaviors. But continuous, noticeable symptoms are indicators that your roommate needs help.

Obsessive-Compulsive Disorder and Your Roommate: A Story

Casey, a senior, was Jessica's third roommate in two years. Jessica's previous relationships had ended badly due to her diagnosed obsessive-compulsive disorder. Because of confidentiality issues, Casey was unaware of Jessica's disorder and only knew that the past two roommates "just did not work out." Also, Casey was carrying a full load of classes and working part-time at the campus coffee shop and did not spend much time in the dorm room. If she did, it was to sleep or study.

"At first, I just thought Jessica had a thing about germs. She was always washing her hands, which were red and chapped. I asked if she wanted to use some of my hand lotion, but she said 'no.' We lived in a suite with a small kitchenette. One night while I was studying, I noticed she was doing this weird thing at the kitchen sink. She would wipe her hands, which were dry, on a paper towel, and then cover the faucet handles with a clean paper towel before turning on the water. She would wash her hands over and over, dry them, wipe off the faucet handle and repeat the same thing. I could not imagine her hands being that dirty but I had never really noticed any of this before, so I was curious. The next night, it was the same thing. Since I did not get back from class and work until dinner time, I did not see her doing this during the day. It was not just the number of times she washed her hands that was strange, but it was the step-by-step routine. It was as if she were a robot.

"I had heard of OCD from my mom, who is a teacher. One of the kids in her class had it, but she did not talk about it much. I just remembered her saying that this girl would arrange and re-arrange her pencils on her desk and be oblivious to anything else going on around her. I wanted to see if Jessica even knew she was doing it, so in the middle of her hand-washing routine, I asked, 'Jessica, why do you keep washing your hands? They are going to be really chapped.'

She did not blink an eye and said she knew there were lots of germs around and did not want to get sick.

I started to notice other weird things she did like getting up a million times to check to see if her laptop was shut down or if the door was locked. I wanted to yell, 'Stop checking the stupid door!' but did not because in a way, I felt sorry for her. It must be exhausting and embarrassing to act like that. Plus, it was not as if I was around a lot, although it did get on my nerves when I was there. After a while, I did not even notice it. It was just who she was. I did, at one point, ask her if she knew about obsessive-compulsive disorder and she denied knowing anything about it. I was too busy to try to be her therapist, so I just went about my business, trying to get through to graduation. I do not know what ever happened to her, but I think of her every now and then."

> **KIM:** The transition to college is stressful for everyone but is heightened for those suffering from anxiety-related disorders.

How to Help A Roommate Who Cannot Help Herself

You and your parents have worked hard to get to this point. Depending on your choice of colleges, someone is shelling out between $10,000 and $40,000 a year for you to get an education. Higher education is a major investment not only in money, but personal growth and your future. Are you willing to spend a portion of this short time playing nurse or caretaker to a roommate with a mental illness or substance-abuse problem?

Or are you solely focused on getting good grades, preparing for graduation or seeking professional employment? You may be someone who has little time or concern for a roommate who binges, abuses drugs, or is constantly depressed. This does not mean you are a bad person. For some students who come from a family of modest means, spending more time in college beyond four years is simply not an option. If you will have student loans upon graduating and take that responsibility seriously, you will be focused on getting good grades and securing a job after graduation. Students who do not have the time or inclination to play caretaker should seek the help of an RD when their roommate's chronic mental-health problem starts to negatively affect their daily lives and ability to study and stay focused on academics.

For those who want to try to help, know that denial, shame, and embarrassment are some of the reasons people suffering from mental-health issues do not seek help. Educating yourself on the perceived problem before trying to initiate an empathetic conversation will provide informed guidelines and boundaries. Offer gentle, nonjudgmental support and listen to what they have to say, even though it may be a new experience to you or provides a level of discomfort.

You can encourage them to seek help but do not be surprised of your offer is met with continued resistance. People can have preconceived reasons why they should not seek counseling or why it would not work for them. They may think counselors have their own problems or that it is too expensive. They may think counselors are only interested in prescribing medication or delving into childhood experiences that have little to do with the present, when those experiences may be directly linked to the problem. People can also be critical of counseling because they consider therapists "strangers" whom they cannot trust, rather than viewing them as trained professionals. Also, to most people, there is a level of discomfort in talking about a behavior of which they are ashamed. They would have to first admit there is a problem and many cannot even get to that first step.

You can help debunk the myths of counseling by assuring your roommate that it is confidential and helping her find out if the cost is covered by insurance. However, like any mental-health issue your roommate may be experiencing, you cannot hold her hand all of the time. She has to be willing to address the problem, acknowledge it and eventually seek help on her own.

> **KIM:** People may be opposed to seeking professional counseling for a variety of reasons, including cost, confidentiality, and preconceived notions not based on fact or experience. Another reason is denial. They are less likely to seek help when they cannot recognize there is a problem.

Counseling Services

College life brings opportunities and presents challenges that can be overwhelming. Students are encountering new situations for the first times in their lives — living away from home, deciding on an academic major, making new relationships, experiencing exam anxiety, and adjusting to a life style that may be quite different from what they experienced at home. Add to that struggles they may have with family and relationship issues, and stress is even more rampant. While students turn to family and friends for support, the issues they are facing can be more effectively addressed with the help of professionals.

Student-counseling services exist to help students cope with personal, emotional, and situational barriers to learning; improve students' adjustment to stress; and contribute to their personal growth and development by providing psychological support. Services are available from psychologists, social workers, and psychiatrists. Educational and prevention services are also available and may include workshops, online resources, outreach events, mediation, and conflict coaching. Mental health screenings, workshops on family relationships, group therapy, counseling services especially designed for women, and cultural-specific services may also be available.

Counseling services will work in tandem with other offices, such as student health, multicultural affairs, student affairs, and student services to assist enrolled students. There is either no charge or minimal fees for services as the cost may be included in other annual fees. Consultations are offered before arranging for ongoing counseling. All consultations and counseling sessions are confidential.

Some common reasons students seek out on-campus counseling include:

- Anxiety

- Depression

- Experiencing difficulty keeping up with work/not getting expected grades

- Feeling excluded from peer groups

- Homesickness

- End of a relationship

- Family issues

- Eating disorder, self-injury, substance abuse

7

Conflict, Cooperation, and Compromise

You will encounter conflict throughout your life, in personal and professional relationships, with neighbors, friends, family members, and even college roommates. It is human nature to hold different points of view and not see eye to eye with people, whether they are strangers or someone you have known your entire life. But it is possible to hold a conflicting point of view and not let it affect your relationships. This is the kind of situation that is bound to arise with your roommate. You will likely have different religious, life style, political, and ethical views.

One approach is to try to address and resolve the conflict as soon as it happens. You may have heard about married couples who say they never go to bed angry with each other. It may not be as easy as that when you have your first run-in with your roommate, but the longer you let the problem go, the higher the tension level and chance for miscommunication.

But when personality dynamics come into play, things can get sticky. A stalemate can be reached in which neither party is willing to budge. That is when the "troops" are called in to help set realistic goals and facilitate a productive discussion. In your case, you have the advantage of having the "troops" in your building, and their service is free of charge. Resident directors (RDs) and resident assistants (RAs) are specifically trained in conflict resolution and well versed in the issues facing college students. In this chapter, we will examine different situations based on actual college roommate experiences, as well as resolution strategies and strategies to avoid conflict before it becomes an issue.

Conflict or Friendly Disagreement?

There are classic cases of people in and out of the public eye who are in successful relationships but disagree on fundamental issues, be they political or religious. California Governor Arnold Schwarzenegger is a lifelong Republican while his wife, Maria Shriver, is Democrat who comes from one of the most highly visible line of Democrats in the country's history: the Kennedy family. Pundits James Carville (Democrat) and Mary Matalin (conservative Republican) are married and appear regularly on TV's political talk-show circuit. Even the Sunday morning political roundtable members offer opposite points of view but are clearly sometimes enjoying each other's company and are friends off the set. In these examples, the conflicts have little to do with each other's personalities but more so the issues for which each person feels strongly about.

If you think you have encountered a conflict with your roommate, try to separate the issue from the personality. Ask yourself if the conflict has to do with the way your roommate is behaving, including habits you may find annoying, or if it is an inherent personality trait, such as whining or gossiping. Think about your desired outcome and how you can bring that about. Attacking someone's personality versus asking them to correct a behavior will make a difference in whether your desired outcome is achieved.

When you do not see eye to eye with your roommate, it is all right to agree to disagree. You may not agree with their viewpoint or opinion, but part of being an adult is to accept and respect different points of view, especially if you value the relationship.

Pete and Rob got along great. They joined the same fraternity their first year on campus and hung out with a group of friends they met through Habitat for Humanity. But Rob considered Pete to be a slob. Rob was not obsessed with cleanliness but liked order in their small dorm room and was constantly calling Pete a "pig" or a "slob:"

Rob: *"Pete, look at these dishes in the sink. You're a pig."*

Is it Pete's personality that is causing the conflict over cleanliness or a behavioral trait? Is it correctable or an inherent component of who Pete is? It would be easy for Pete to correct the situation by washing the dishes, not just once to please Rob but on a regular basis. Correcting this behavior would lessen tension between the two of them. But calling Pete a name is going to have little effect on whether he is willing to correct his behavior, as it is a personal attack. Explaining to Pete why his behavior is annoying and why you want him to correct it (your desired outcome) is more likely to bring about change:

"Pete, can you please wash your dishes so I can use the sink?"

Here there is no name-calling, and Rob is asking him to correct his behavior and explaining why using an "I" statement: *so I can use the sink*. This approach lets Pete know that his behavior has a direct effect on Rob. Personality traits, as discussed in Chapter 3, are more deeply embedded and challenging to try to change as they can cause ongoing and irresolvable conflict.

> **KIM:** When encountering what you think is a conflict with your roommate, ask yourself if it is based on behavior that can be corrected or personality that is embedded in that person's character.

Causes of Conflict

What situations can cause roommate conflict? The list, unfortunately, is long. Keeping in mind that a roommate relationship is, in many ways, similar to a romantic relationship, some root causes have to do with living together on a daily basis and seeing each other's best and worst attributes. What complicates things even further, is that it all takes place in a small space. The most common causes of college roommate conflict include:

- Noise

- Lack of respect for roommate's study/sleep time

- Overnight guests or guests staying too long

- Drug or alcohol use

- Cleanliness or lack thereof

- Sharing, borrowing, or taking personal belongings

- Different life styles

- Cultural clashes

When Tension Builds

When tension builds between people due to a conflict, the recipient of the door slams, silence, and dirty looks is not always aware of the problem. If you are suddenly the recipient of the "cold-shoulder" treatment from your roommate, try to get her to verbalize what is going on. You probably do not want to ask outright if she is angry with you as that implies there may be a reason. She may be having a problem with a relationship, classes, or her family, so there is a chance it has nothing to do with you. But if you find her behavior is directly affecting your comfort level with her, it is best not to ignore it. You may try this approach:

"I noticed you have been quiet lately. Is something going on?"

This opens the door for her to share or respond directly if the reason for a tense environment has to do with you. If the response is, "I do not want to talk about it," the reason is either private or because the situation is about your relationship and she does not want to address it. A good response from you would be:

"All right. If you do want to talk at some point, I am here to listen."

But if the tension gets worse and is not resolved, there is definitely something going on between you two, and ignoring it increases the tension level. The unresolved conflict could lead to feeling angry, or resentful. Living in a tense environment, whether it is in a romantic or family relationship, is never healthy for anyone.

If you have a complaint about or gripe with your roommate, verbalize it before your anger builds and the tension increases to an intolerable level. The longer you wait to address conflict, the more difficult it becomes to address it because of the time that has passed. However, never try to address conflict in a state of heightened emotion. (This is also advice to carry over into personal relationships.) There is a higher chance that you, or the other person, will say something hurtful that cannot be taken back with an apology.

Also, beware of the "anger explosion" that can occur when people have narcissistic personality traits. They will say, "That does not bother me," when their anger grows and grows until it explodes into an all-out argument. Almost everyone knows someone with this personality trait. He or she seems laid-back and easygoing but something is eating away at them. When his or her anger over the situation builds and builds, he or she goes off on a tirade and issues or conflicts from many years past come up as well. That behavior leaves the other person in a no-win situation. If he or she tries to combat the anger, he or she ends up screaming along with the other person. If he or she tries to explain the situation or tries to defend himself or herself, someone in a heightened emotional state is not going to hear it. If he or she tries to get the other person refocused on the issue at hand, he or she could anger the individual even further.

KIM: If you have a complaint or gripe with your roommate, verbalize it before your anger builds and the situation escalates.

The Engaged Listener

One way to try and diffuse someone's anger when he or she is in a state of heightened emotion is to listen until he or she calms down. Your initial reaction and built-in response is to start to explain your point of view or scream back. When someone is angry, there is a good chance he or she will not hear you or anyone else, so trying to reason with him or her is most likely not going to have a positive affect.

Each person wants to be heard during a disagreement. Talking or screaming at the same time will not accomplish anything productive. A person who excels at communication is someone who listens to the other person's point of view and absorbs what he or she is saying before speaking.

Emphatic listeners, however, do not apologize or agree with another point of view just to get beyond the ranting, especially if they disagree. When the person ranting calms down, you can try to have a rational conversation with her. If you do not think this is possible at that time, tell her you will be happy to discuss the issue later when she is not angry. If, at any time, you feel threatened or in physical danger by her behavior, leave the scene, even if it means leaving your room.

This is why, as mentioned earlier, you want to try to verbally address the conflict when there is someone present who is outside the situation. That would be an RD, RA, or even a graduate student on the housing staff. Someone there to mediate will set guidelines and allow everyone equal time to present their case and vent. All that person may want is a forum to express his or her feelings to anyone who will listen.

If you encounter a verbal conflict with your roommate or if she is yelling or being verbally abusive, you are in a position to make an informed choice: be an active listener or walk away from the situation. Walking away can be problematic if the encounter happened in your room, but if you can get away for a while, even going down the hall and telling a hall mate that you needed a break from your roommate, this will give her time to defuse. If the situation has escalated upon your return, or if she picks up where she left off, go to your RD who will intercede. Always keep in mind that your safety and welfare should be your No. 1 priority while living in a residence hall. When someone is in the middle of an angry rant, he or she could act unreasonably without giving it a second thought.

> **KIM:** When a roommate is angry and verbally taking it out on you, acknowledge what he is saying by responding with "All right," "Ummm hmm" or a nod of the head.

Strategies for Listening and Responding

To be an active listener, show with your body, facial expression, and verbal response that you hear what he or she is saying.

You can nod your head on occasion or say "yes" or "uhmmm hmmm" to show that you acknowledge and empathize with what he or she is saying, even if the other person is ranting and saying things that are untrue. Addressing the person by name will also show her that you are paying attention and aware of her emotional state. She most likely will not take note of your respectful behavior at the moment, but at least you acted in a reasonable and mature manner. The tone and volume of your voice are important as well. One tactic to quell a rant from your roommate is to repeat what she is saying, using "I" and "you" along with rephrasing her words.

For example, say your roommate has been having problems with her family. In the same week, she failed two exams and knows if she does not pick up her grades, she will lose her scholarship. She is angry at herself and her family. She left the door unlocked and when you came back from class; it was wide open. Luckily, nothing was missing, but this is not the first time you had to remind her to lock up.

You: *You left the door unlocked again and it was wide open when I came back from class.*

(You are stating a fact and your point of view without anger or accusation.)

Roommate: *You criticize everything I do. No matter what I do, it is just not good enough for you. I cannot stand living with you anymore. I want out . . . I want out of here. I don't ever want to see you again . . .*

You: *All right* . . . (you are acknowledging, but not agreeing, to what she is saying.)

Roommate: *Didn't you hear what I said? You are not even listening to me. You never listen to what I have to say.*

You: *I am listening, Emily. I'm right here, listening to you.*

(You are affirming that you hear her. You address her by name.)

You let her rant for a while and she calms down. There is some silence.

You: *I understand it has been a tough week for you. You are saying that I criticize everything you do, but both of us know that is not true. I realize that you are upset right now and may not realize what you are saying.*

(You are using "you" and "I" to personalize the situation. You let her know you are empathetic to her dilemma, but you have also stated your point of view — that she left the door unlocked and that is unacceptable behavior.)

Another useful tactic to derail a rant is to address the person by name and to ask questions to help your roommate regain focus. We have all been emotional at times and will ramble, repeat ourselves, and not make sense. Some emotional outbursts happen even when one has planned out what he or she is going to say. In a situation of heightened emotions, another person's reaction can trigger an outburst and unreasonable behavior. On the television show, "Intervention," family and friends confront a loved one with a list of what they want to say. Even though the interventionists have the best intentions, the response of their loved one will throw them off track, causing them to cry and not be able to follow through, and their loved one often becomes verbally caustic or storms out of the room.

By combining a few tactics, you not only gather additional information about what the other person is saying, but you help him or her to focus on his or her words, no matter how unreasonable. In the example below, you are combining these tactics:

- Addressing the person by name

- Asking specific questions to gather more information

- Stating your point of view or position in a calm manner

- Using "I" and "you"

Roommate: *You told Jason I was sleeping with Paul and then he gossiped to the whole floor. Now everyone knows what I am doing. Everyone knows about this and it is going to ruin my life . . .*

You: *Jen. What are you talking about?*

(You are addressing her by name. Asking question to clarify.)

Roommate: *You know what I am talking about. You are the one who started this whole thing.*

You: *What thing did I start?*

(You are asking specific question.)

Roommate: *Don't pretend like you don't know.*

You: *Do you mean I started this rumor?*

(Using question to clarify accusation.)

Roommate: *Well, who else would have started it? It is just what you wanted. I know it is . . .*

You: *Jen, I don't really understand what it is you're talking about, but I assure you that I haven't started a rumor about you. I don't believe in gossip.*

(You address her by name again. You directly address the issue and deny it.)

She could continue to rant at this point, but you have stated your position and made it clear (even though she did not make sense) that you are not responsible for her emotional state.

> **KIM:** When confronted by an angry roommate, be an active listener, ask questions to help her stay focused, address her by name, and state your position in a calm and reasonable voice.

When You Are the One Who is Angry

As mentioned earlier, it is part of human nature to react emotionally when someone verbally attacks you, your behavior, or your character. When someone's emotions erupt without notice, you do not have time to strategize about how you will react. Your initial response may be shock, anger, or hurt. But if you are the one to explode in an angry tirade, try to heed the warning signs to head off your behavior before you say something you will later regret.

If you can remove yourself from the situation, do so. If you can ask for some time to think the situation over, do so. For example, your roommate is a slob. He leaves dirty clothes, leftover food and takeout containers all over the room. You have asked him a million times to please clean up after himself, but he does not. You see this as a sign of disrespect for a space that is yours as well as his. You come home late after a chem lab. You are tired, hungry and in a bad mood. You step on an open pizza box the minute you open the door. He is sleeping, but you do not care. You immediately go into a tirade, pick up the box and throw it at him. You "see red" and start yelling, calling him a slob and a thoughtless idiot. You say that you cannot take this anymore — that you cannot live in this situation anymore and then threaten to move out. You slam the door. Then what? It is your room. What are the consequences? Where will you go?

When You Are the One at Fault

If you have breached your roommate's confidence, broken a rule, or behaved inappropriately, and recognize this to be the case, it is up to you to apologize and initiate resolution. Any kind of conflict with another person brings a level of discomfort, but you can learn about yourself from the experience and in some cases, deepen the relationship. Tell him that you acknowledge your behavior was wrong and that you will make every effort not to repeat it. Here is an example:

"Jamie, I know we agreed not to share each other's laptops and what I did was wrong, so I apologize. I hope you accept my apology and you have my reassurance that this will not happen again."

"I see your point of view and that I misjudged the situation. I do not want to argue anymore. I want to move on."

After that, you need to stick to your guns and not repeat that behavior. Let us assume you had your roommate's trust at the beginning of the relationship and want to regain it. Another way to win back your roommate's trust is to show that you are willing and able to see his point of view and demonstrate that you want the relationship to work.

If you and your roommate are angry over something but neither of you remember what it was exactly that caused the conflict or are not sure who caused it, it is best to compromise and share the blame. In personal relationships, this often happens. There will be a disagreement that leaves both parties angry and hurt. Then time passes and neither party can recall what the problem was. If you know you are the one who caused the conflict, take ownership of it.

Here are some suggested conversation-starters to get beyond the problem, whatever it may have been, and put it behind you:

"I don't know about you, but I'm not even sure what we're arguing about anymore. Can we just move on?"

"I agree that we need to address this problem and work it out."

"I know I can be pushy sometimes and you have every right to point it out to me."

"I am willing to work things out and come up with a fair compromise."

Conflict Resolution Primer

Your roommate does not have to be your best friend or even your friend. But you do want a relationship based on mutual respect. Even if you think you get along beautifully with your roommate, at some point in your college career, conflict will arise. It could take the form of a fight over who drank the last can of Red Bull that is quickly resolved with an apology and stocking the fridge with new energy drinks. It could take the form of a misunderstanding about a previous agreement that results in a few tense days during which no one speaks, but then one person reaches out to the other and both cannot recall what the issue was. The most effective remedy for conflict is communication. When countries are at a hostile standoff, talks among leaders are encouraged. When a marriage breaks down, couples seek therapy to open the lines of communication. Even on elementary school playgrounds, when conflict is a daily issue, the resolution entails communication between teachers and students and then the students to each other.

Assuming that someone knows how you feel and what you want to say can lead to miscommunication and misinterpretation. Spell it out for them. For example,

Roommate #1: *"You said you never wanted to see my face again."*

Roommate #2: *"You should have known I was exaggerating."*

Roommate #1: *"How was I supposed to know what you meant?"*

Is it possible to completely avoid conflict with your roommate(s) throughout your college career? Yes, it is possible and I spoke to many current and former students who claim that was the case. When I asked if they ever had an argument, the answer was always "yes." When I asked if there was ever tension or if they ever got on each other's nerves, again, the answer was "yes." Did these minor glitches get in the way of these roommates getting along and surviving in the same space for four years? Not for them.

However, let us assume, in the spirit of being prepared, that you will encounter a major conflict with your roommate. The next few chapters will provide some tips and insights into conflict recognition and resolution, but let us first look at some strategies to head off conflict before it arises.

If you have taken the time to get to know your roommate, including his habits, likes and dislikes, schedule, and cultural and family background, you will have a better sense of who he is, which will help you implement these general guidelines when conflict arises.

- Do not wait until the situation is intolerable.

- Get all parties involved and in the same room.

- Do not invite friends or anyone who is outside of the situation.

- Take turns describing the conflict. Talk in calm tones.

Complicated conflicts between roommates can be based on differences, similarities, misunderstandings, and lack of regard or respect for the other person. Those are the conflicts that will take more time and energy to resolve than you may expect to invest, but like any relationship, it will take some work.

Before we get into the nitty-gritty of conflict resolution, here are some basic guidelines:

- All parties involved should agree to meet

- A mediator should lead the discussion. This person should not be part of the conflict, but rather an RA

- Try to meet in a neutral location (not in your hall room)

- Everyone should be at the same eye-level, either all seated or all on the floor

There are several goals in planning a meeting to try to resolve conflicts. You want to respect everyone's point of view in the same way you want your's respected. You also want to come to some kind of an agreement. It may take several meetings to get there, but think of that as your ultimate goal. Do you need a signed agreement rather than a verbal one? Finally, you need to come to an agreement on actions necessary to bring about change.

Each person takes a turn stating his or her side to the story. This is the hard part. Try to state your side without demonstrating anger, without crying, without blame, and without malice. You will read this over and over in this section: Use "I" and "you" throughout. This is crucial in communicating the issues. State what the offense is. Also state how your roommate's action made you feel. State the reason that you think your roommate did whatever she did. Then state the resolution you would like to see.

What was the offense? Your "you" statement:

You did _____. You said _____.

How did it make you feel? Your "I" statement:

I was _____ when you _____. I felt (angry, hurt, left out) _____ when you _____.

Why I believe you did or said that.

You must have been _____ when you did that.

You must have done that because you felt _____.

What resolution do you desire? What action needs to be taken to resolve the conflict?

What I would like us to do is _____. What I need from you is _____.

KIM: Three major goals in resolving conflict:

1. Be respectful of everyone's point of view.

2. All parties need to come to an agreement.

3. All parties need to agree on actions necessary to bring about resolution.

Communicating the Problem

Controlling emotions when confronting the person with whom you have a conflict is the first step in successful resolution. Anyone who has argued with a friend or family member, which means almost everyone, can recall the point when a confluence of emotions came together and resulted in pent-up anger, jealousy, and mistrust. When this happens, things are said, accusations are made, and reasoning is clouded by heightened emotions. If you and your roommate come head-to-head over an issue, or several issues, there is bound to be an argument at some point and what makes the "walking-away" approach more difficult is that you can only do so temporarily; you both have to live in the same space. But walking away from roommate confrontation is all right if you have intentions of readdressing the problem. Take a break. Cool down and come back to try again. Take stock of what this relationship means to you. If you see your roommate only in passing because you are both busy, how much time and energy do you want to invest in resolving conflict? If you like your roommate but are just going through a rough patch, make the effort. Take a look at how you may be responsible for what is happening and do some soul-searching.

So, you have decided the relationship is worth salvaging. You want to resolve the conflict but you are both angry and no one is talking. Now you have to come up with a way to communicate with your roommate in an effective, empathetic and understanding way. And you need to do it face-to-face to be successful.

The Dangers of E-mail and Telephone

E-mail can convey words and conserve time but it cannot convey verbal signals, which are key to successful and meaningful communication. E-mail also makes it easy to vent anger and frustration, but unless you take a few moments and re-read what you wrote or wait until the next day to see if your feelings have changed, once you press "send," there is no getting it back. Communicating by phone provides verbal signals which convey emotion and tone, but lacks eye contact. Both methods cannot convey key signals that not only connect people in relationships, but are useful when confronting or resolving conflict: body language, eye contact, hand movement and facial expression. Even the way you sit or stand during conversation, whether it is friendly or confrontational, tells the other person something about yourself and your feelings in addition to the words you use.

Today's college students instant-message their friends about everything. It is not only a communication tool that defines their generation, but one well within their comfort level. Used to convey the most minute, personal information, it is no surprise that e-mail or messaging is the delivery method most students will prefer to use when communicating a problem to their roommate. But returning e-mails with tones of increasing anger and frustration still leaves an unsolved problem and even further creates a void of communication. Unless you are an exceptional communicator, you will not be able to resolve conflict through text messaging. You can perhaps come to some kind of temporary truce, such as, "All right. I'll never sit on your bed again," but the tone in that example alone insinuates a hidden message: "I'll do this now to make you shut up, but promise that I'll never sit on your bed again? Get real." The issues at the base of the conflict are still there — looming around the corner — only to be solved by an actual conversation.

The Dangers of E-mail and Telephone: A Story

"I grew up in a big family," said Mark, a sophomore in Boston. "We had lively conversations at dinner and my mom, who was a history professor, would quiz us on current events. It sounds a little strange now, but we all developed really good conversational skills. I text-message my friends, or, I should say they text me, but I think too much gets lost in translation, if you know what I mean. My roommate and I got along great our first year but then he started bringing his boyfriend back to our room. Boyfriends, I should say. He had just come out to his friends and family and it was as if he were a poster child for reckless behavior. I made it clear from the get-go that I had no problem with his life style, but I had a problem with them going at it in the middle of the night. I need my sleep."

"Then the text messages started. One after another, accusing me of being homophobic, snobbish, privileged, you name it. It was like a third-grade game of name-calling — blowing the whole thing out of proportion and creating a fictional situation through text messages. The worse part is he was copying all of these messages to his friends and writing about me on his blog, and not in a good way. Then I started getting nasty messages from his friends, almost all of whom I had never even met. How unfair was this to me? The only thing I was guilty of was wanting to have a one-on-one conversation with him, and since I didn't see him for days after this started happening, I didn't have a chance to talk to him. Because I refused to text him back, he took that to mean I wanted nothing to do with him, and he texted me, telling me so."

"I didn't know what else to do, so I left a note saying I wasn't angry and I wanted to work things out, but would only do so if we sat down and talked. I had to do this a few more times before he seemed to calm down and said all right. We agreed on a time and place — his favorite Chinese restaurant down the block. I thought getting in his good graces would make the conversation easier and I was right. He apologized immediately and admitted he had been a jerk. He said he had come out too quickly and wasn't prepared for the backlash, which evidently he was getting from some close friends. He was paranoid and defensive and jumped at any chance to defend himself, which he didn't have to do with me. I told him all he had to do was mention all of this to me to my face, and it would have saved a lot of hurt feelings. Everything worked out and he even picked up the tab for dinner."

If leaving a note or e-mailing a proposed time and place to meet helps break the ice, then go for it, but do not expect your conflict to be resolved through cute emoticons and sentences all in lower case. Every difficult and uncomfortable conversation you have with your roommate, or other college friends, will better prepare you for what is in store in marriage, relationships, partnerships, parenting, and your professional career.

KIM: Confronting your roommate over conflict can only be successful if done so in person, face-to-face, where both of your can convey verbal and physical signals that are crucial to successful communication.

Acting Responsibly Versus Reacting Irresponsibly

If you are the type of person who becomes defensive when someone finds your action or behavior offensive, you will find a reason within the first few days why you cannot live with your roommate. Avoiding the issues, blaming others, and assuming your view is the right one will bring attention to your stay in a hall. The RDs will come to know you. The housing office will come to know you, and everyone on your floor will come to know you — and I do not mean in a good way. If you take the issue of conflict to your parents, they will either tell you to learn to handle it on your own, or pick up the phone and demand to speak to the housing director. Conferring with your parents or seeking their advice is a good idea, but unless you are being threatened or feel unsafe, this is your problem. Just like the cell phone and credit card bills are yours to handle.

College students live in a more insular environment than even a decade ago. They are constantly connected with friends through cell phones and personal-communication devices and often drown out their surroundings through iPods and iPhones. When something comes up during the course of their day, they are likely to immediately IM or text-message a friend or call a parent to complain. If they do not like the way a professor talked to them in class, they will call Mom. The smallest conflict can become overwhelming to them because they do not have the negotiation, communication, and social skills of previous generations, during which people talked face-to-face to resolve conflicts. In other words, today's college students are more likely to react immediately to a situation rather than take time to digest the problem and figure out a way to resolve it. They are also part of a generation that tends to have fewer face-to-face encounters with professors, peers, and people. Facial expression, body language, and tone of voice cannot be conveyed through e-mails.

Also, before you share the conflict with an administration member, do not forget to share it with your roommate first. One college counselor told me that he is often visited by a student with a roommate problem only to find out that the student has never communicated the problem directly to the roommate. Not only that, but the student had text-messaged all of his friends to let them know he was going to the RD about his problem, not thinking that many of those friends were also friends with the roommate and had alerted him, which caused even more tension between the two.

Do not let your emotions take control of your actions. If you encounter a blow-up with your roommate, take a walk, exercise, go somewhere to be around friends or do something to distract yourself for a while. If you truly feel you are not at fault, there is a good chance your roommate will apologize on your return. If the blow-up is over an ongoing matter, you need to sit down and try to resolve it. If it is the result of a more serious problem that cannot be resolved, let your roommate know you plan to seek outside guidance. See if he agrees. Look into mediation or conflict-resolution services available on campus. If you go the RD, ask your roommate if he would like to come along. These are the right steps toward resolution.

KIM: Today's college students rely on text messaging and IM to share problems and conflicts with friends and families rather than face-to-face meetings. They may be more likely to react to a troubling situation immediately, without taking time to think it through, get the other side of the story, or try to resolve it on their own.

When to Call in a Third Party

When attempts to resolve a conflict on your own have failed, and you have exhausted options and tried more than once to talk through the problem, it is time to involve an objective third party. If your first inclination is to bring in a mutual friend, reconsider. This could result in a loss of friendship as your roommate will feel outnumbered and that the friend is siding with you. If you feel you made valid attempts to calmly discuss the conflict and provided possible resolutions, but he still will not cooperate, let him know you have no other alternative but to tell the RD. Invite him with you as this might help resolve the conflict. An exception to this would be if you feel your safety is being compromised and the situation is an emergency. Then you should go directly to the RD without feeling you need to first inform your roommate. If you find out your roommate is complaining about you behind your back, a face-to-face confrontation is best. Let him know you would rather hear the complaints from him — that it is not fair to you.

When you get to this point, explain the situation to the RD and be specific about how you have tried to resolve it on your own and what your roommate's response has been. What you do not want to do is demand action from the RD or threaten to bring in a higher-level authority or even worse, your parents. The problem will only be redirected back to the RD. The RD will determine whether the problem is fixable. Let your RD know you want your roommate to be part of the discussion and stress your interest in resolving the conflict rather than saying you will just move into another dorm.

Student-counseling services may provide direct meditation or conflict-resolution services to help you resolve conflict. To be proactive, attend a conflict-resolution workshop. The RD, housing office, or counseling services can also give you feedback and advice on resolving conflict. These are trained professionals who deal with students with myriad problems, complaints, and issues, so take advantage of their expertise. There is no reason for you to reinvent the wheel and try to get through this on your own.

KIM: If you feel there is no other alternative but to take the problem to the resident staff, tell your roommate you are doing so and invite him or her to come along so both sides of the story are heard, and you are not later accused of doing something behind his back.

Warning! Do Not Ignore

There are situations in which you should not attempt to discuss the conflict or opt for resolution. These situations are any that invovle danger to you or your good standing as a dorm resident. Go directly to your RD if any of the following occur:

- Verbal, physical, or sexual abuse or harassment

- If your roommate is stealing any of your personal belongings

- If you roommate is misusing or abusing residence hall property

- Illegal-substance abuse

- Substance abuse that is not illegal, but impeding your ability to live with your roommate

- Guests of your roommate that compromise your living situation

- Your roommate discussing or attempting suicide or self-harm

- Health situations that require emergency care

Signs of depression and suicidal behavior are discussed in previous sections of this book.

8

When to Call it Quits

When all options have been exhausted, the last resort is to move on. That is, one or both of you has to move out of the room. It is the last resort for the housing office and the university as well. It may well cost them, your parents, and yourself money and expend time and resources, especially if you are the one responsible for the move. If you believe the move is required because your roommate is "a jerk," "a slob," or a "clean freak," do not embarrass yourself by saying so. Those are not valid reasons for a move. They are just facts of life that you need to live with. However, if a situation arises in which your safety is compromised, your belongings are being stolen, your roommate is conducting illegal activities, or there is a proven invasion of your privacy, then you have every right to want to end this relationship.

Find out the university's policy on moving out of your dorm room, whether it is the middle or end of the semester. You can find this either on the housing agreement you signed or through the housing office. If you and your roommate both agree a move is necessary and if one of you volunteers to move, it will make the transition easier for everyone. If neither of you volunteers, the housing office will intercede. However, that office cannot perform miracles, and it is likely there will not be any rooms available, especially in the middle of the semester or mid-academic year. You and your roommate can spread the word and see if anyone else is looking to switch roommates, but that will require cooperation and there is a chance lack of cooperation got you into this situation to begin with.

Saying good-bye may not be an option if the relationship ended because your roommate was violent, abusive, or breaking the law. But if you just could not live with each other, and the housing office was in agreement, there is no reason not to wish each other well, especially if you are around each other when packing. If it is a small campus, there is a good chance you will run into each other again. That can happen on the largest of campuses, too. Acknowledge that things did not work out and tell him you hope it does with the next roommate.

If your roommate just cannot let her anger or resentment go and feels the need to keep bringing it up until the last T-shirt is packed, wave your hand, say good-bye, and walk out. You can try telling her you "do not want to revisit what happened and just want to move on," but if she persists in reminding you of everything you ever did to annoy her, you are under no obligation to listen or respond. If you were friends at one time, this may be hurtful and certainly not the way you wanted the relationship to end, but you may be glad to see your roommate go.

Can We Still be Friends?

What if you lie about why you requested a move? One of the reasons it is best to be honest with your roommate about why you moved out is that you may get that person to realize they were difficult to live with. With a few exceptions, most people do not like confrontation, and we all avoid it or put it off if possible, making excuses or just dreading the possibility of hurting someone's feelings. But if you lie about the reasons you requested a move and assume that out of 25,000 students you will never run into him, think again. One student told me she could not bring herself to tell her ex-roommate she requested a move because of her poor hygiene. So she lied and said she was transferring to another college. Sure enough, she ran into her on campus and lied again, telling her ex that she changed her mind at the last minute.

There will and have been many instances in which former roommates not only remain friends, but look back on whatever the conflict was and either laugh, scratch their heads, or feel embarrassed that it ever got to the point of wanting to separate. You are only 18 when you start college, and you have a whole different perspective on what is important by the time graduation rolls around or if graduate school is on the horizon. Arguing over leaving wet towels on the floor seems childish when you are studying for the LSATs and your future may depend on how well you test.

KIM: How your relationship ends with your roommate when a move is required can take several directions. You can part friends, enemies, or somewhere in between. You may never see that person again or reconnect later on. Either way, you have learned something about human nature and yourself.

Next Steps

Your college stay is brief and your energy should be spent on getting an education and experiencing new opportunities rather than on a roommate situation that for whatever reasons, is not going to improve or go away on its own. What happens and where you go next depends on you. Evaluate the situation. If this is not your first move, take a look at what costs will be incurred to move again. Have you lost a deposit? Will it cost to pack up and move somewhere else on campus. There will definitely be costs incurred if you move off campus. Is the situation that serious? Do you have to move, even if it will cost you and your parents money? You have no guarantee the next roommate will be any better than the one you are moving away from. As previously noted, if you feel your safety and well-being are being compromised in any way, and you need to move out immediately, then additional costs are a secondary concern.

If your final decision is to move, you should be proactive. If you roommate said he would be the one to move and changes his mind, you may be stuck with no place else to live for the rest of that semester. If you have worked things out with the housing office and there is a mutual agreement between them and yourself, find out what resources are offered to help you find another opening. See if there is a waiting list for students looking for roommates. Is there an online resource at the university to post your request?

The first place to search for off-campus housing is actually on-campus through the housing office. Almost all universities have an off-campus housing section within the housing Web site. There are also plenty of other Web databases listing people looking for on- and off-campus roommates or roommates looking for other roommates. One that specializes in college roommates is **www.campusroommates.com**, which includes a comprehensive listing of ads that are specific to a college or university, such as:

Seeking roommate for next year — College of St. Catherine

I need a roommate to share 2 BR apartment — Sienna College

Or, you can search by state, city or college to narrow down the field. Another consideration is Craigslist at **www.cragislist.com,** which is widely used by college students. Other roommate search Web sites such as **www.roommates.com** or **www.campusroommates. com.** Also, word of mouth is a good way to see who else is looking for a new roommate.

On one hand, looking for a replacement roommate puts you in a good position: you have experienced the "roommate from hell" and know what to ask and look for in the next one. On the other hand, potential roommates may be suspicious of why you want to move, especially if it is not your first one. They may wonder if the problem is actually with you. Be honest and up-front when you talk to a newly matched roommate. Tell them what happened — whether it was the naked roommate, the drunk roommate, the sex-addict roommate — these indicators should be warning signs to them that you are serious about living in a sane environment and will not tolerate the same craziness as before. Also, there is a good chance you will find someone who moved out of his or her room for the same reasons you did, so you can share war stories.

No matter how proactive you are there is a possibility, depending on what time of year you request a move, that no rooms are available. Your options then are to find temporary off-campus housing, move back home for the rest of the semester if you live close enough, or stick with it until the semester is over.

KIM: If you have exhausted all options and have made a final decision to move to another dorm, be proactive. See what matching services or waiting lists are available through the housing office and take advantage of online postings and word of mouth when shopping for a new roommate.

Off-Campus Housing

Timing can play a role in your final decision to move off-campus. If you leave mid-semester, you may not be able to recoup any deposits or fees paid to the university. If you signed a contract for the full academic year, breaking that contract may incur costs as well. Look over your housing agreement or call the housing office before making this decision. Also keep in mind that you will incur costs to move, including the actual move, security deposit, first and possibly last month's rent, utilities activation, cable/Internet hookup, and other miscellaneous fees. Spring is most likely the best time to start searching for off-campus housing for that fall.

If you have made the decision to live off campus, there are many options from which to choose. Rather than navigate the maze of apartment hunting on your own, your first stop should be the university's housing office, which will most likely have a separate off-campus housing unit. Before you even get to that point, check out the housing Web site by searching for "off-campus housing," or "off-campus living."

Most mid-size to large universities own privately developed and managed anchor properties near campus or within the surrounding community. They could be across the street from campus, within walking distance, or accessible by campus shuttle. They are usually affordable and normally have many amenities, such as pools, gyms and proximity to cultural and historical venues. The university will most likely maintain a list of local apartment complexes and provide services to help you make the transition to off-campus living, such as workshops on understanding leases and one-on-one service.

The staff in the off-campus housing office will provide assistance concerning your legal obligations and those of your landlord, information on rental insurance, safety procedures, and financial aid. They also have developed relationships with landlords, property managers, and real-estate agents and oversee site inspections and property listings before making them available to students. They will also assist you on understanding policies within the lease, such as amount of rent, length of lease, security deposits, and terms and conditions. Just as it was important for you to read and understand the terms of your dorm policy, it is even more important to do the same when living off campus. Many housing offices offer off-campus housing information sessions or fairs.

For your own protection, you and your roommate should inspect the apartment using a checklist before signing any legal document or giving a security deposit. This will ensure that tenants are not held responsible for any damage done by previous residents. If the landlord is unavailable for a walk-through, you should complete this procedure on your own, with your roommate(s). It may be a good idea to have a parent or experienced and trusted adult with you. Also, take dated photographs of any previous damage.

If the housing office or your landlord does not provide a checklist or inspection form, you can create your own that includes items for your inspection or walk-through before signing the rental agreement. A suggested checklist is included in the Appendices. You should insist that the landlord sign the checklist indicating he or she has agreed to the move-in condition of each item you have indicated. If you will not have a roommate, you may want a witness or third party to co-sign the checklist. If you are moving to off-campus housing because of an irresolvable conflict with a roommate, you have already encountered enough conflict and disagreement and want to avoid any possibility of that in your next adventure in independent living. Again, the office of off-campus housing, if there is one at your university, can assist you on this.

Tips for Living Off-Campus

You will no longer have an RD or 24-hour desk staff to help when something goes wrong in your dorm room. If you kept your dorm room door open on the weekends as an invitation for the many friends who walked by, you cannot do that in an apartment. Even if the property is owned and managed by the university, you and your roommate have more responsibilities than when you lived on campus. Here are a few tips to keep in mind:

1. When you leave for winter or spring break, be sure to secure your apartment. Notify your landlord of the dates you will be away and be sure to leave contact information.

2. Remove and toss perishable items from your refrigerator.

3. Take out the trash and make arrangements to have your mail stopped, forwarded or picked up by a friend.

4. Be sure any pets are well-taken care of in your absence.

5. Upon returning, if there are any signs of a break-in, such as an open door or window, call the police immediately. Do not enter your apartment but wait until the police arrive and have them enter before you. You do not know if someone is still in your apartment.

6. During winter months, if you have no heat or the heat is not working properly, call your landlord immediately. The same applies if you have and use central air conditioning during warmer months.

7. Have the campus-shuttle schedule handy, especially during finals when you may be studying late on campus. The university police or office of campus safety should offer an escort service. Have that number handy as well.

8. Remember you are living in a different community. You and your roommate should be respectful of neighbors and observe municipal ordinances such as noise restrictions, party permits, and property maintenance. If you are not familiar with the ordinances, check with the off-campus housing office. If you live in an apartment not owned or managed by the university, ask your landlord.

9. It will be your responsibility to observe regulations for garbage removal, recycling, storage, and sidewalks.

10. If you are thinking of subletting during summer months — a good way to save money while you are away — check with your landlord or university housing office on what the policy is. The university may also be able to help you find a temporary tenant.

Conclusion

I hope this book has provided helpful information on selecting campus housing and being prepared to live in peace with a stranger you will call "roommate." These pages also provide guidance on how to live, or decide not to live, with a problem roommate, from recognizing conflict, attempting to resolve it on your own, and seeking help. The stories, interviews, and summaries from college and post-college roommates provide even more insight into what goes on behind closed doors in dorms around the country. Even if you breeze through your four years of college without one argument, this book will guide you through residential housing so that you are prepared to concentrate on academics, rather than the noisy, obnoxious, disrespectful, self-centered individual you may find yourself sharing a room with.

Keep this book next to your bed, in plain sight, so when the first conflict arises, you will not only have a reference guide on what to do next, but send a message to your roommate that perhaps she or he should flip through the pages as well.

What follows are appendices that include:

- A sample roommate agreement and preference form

- Articles, case studies, tips and documents by and from higher education housing officials at various universities, called "Advice from the Experts." Their insight is invaluable as they live with many of the issues concerning roommates on a daily basis and are well versed in conflict resolution.

- Tips on living with a roommate

- Roommate-conflict and conflict-resolution articles and documents

- Advice on what to bring, not to bring and what to expect

- Articles on depression and conflict resolution

- Two question-and-answer interviews between the author and housing officials covering the most common complaints by roommates, advice for completing roommate preference forms, stories about major conflicts and alternative solutions

- Firsthand case studies and stories from current and post-college roommates who exemplify the title of this book, "The College Roommate from Hell"

- Bibliography and Resources

Appendix A:
Articles on Roommate Living

PENN STATE UNIVERSITY HOUSING OFFICE: ROOMMATE AGREEMENT

www.sa.psu.edu

EXAMINING YOUR DIFFERENCES

You have probably identified some areas in which you and your roommate have different living preferences.

Take some time to discuss these areas and develop strategies that you are both comfortable with to address these differences. Be specific and clear in detailing your thoughts below. Your RA will follow up on the things that you have listed.

Identify different preference(s):

Possible compromise(s):

Discussion-starters for difficult conversations:

When I am doing something that is bothering you, this is how I prefer to be approached...

If problems arise between us, we should approach them by...

Of the items we've discussed today, the most important to me is...

If I am feeling frustrated, this is how you'll know...

PENN STATE UNIVERSITY HOUSING OFFICE: ROOMMATE AGREEMENT

I find it easy/difficult to talk about these things because...

AGREEMENT

I have examined my living preferences with my roommate. We have developed comfortable solutions to address areas in which we have different preferences. I understand that we will not always agree and that we will need to address issues as they arise. I also understand and agree that the strategies detailed here will be the guidelines for living in our room.

Hall: _____ Room: _____

Name (print): _____Name (print):_____

Signature: _____ Signature:_____
___

Date: _____　　　　Date: _____

Identifying your priorities for comfortable living

The purpose of this contract is to give individuals sharing a room the opportunity to examine each other's personal styles and preferences for living.

We encourage you to set aside some time to discuss the following questions with your roommate(s). By dedicating adequate time to these questions now, you may avoid conflicts in the future.

Take the time together to complete this contract and explain each of your responses. Be as honest and specific as possible.

Remember...communication is the key to the success of your living experience at Penn State.

Roommate name _____

☐ I have shared a room before　☐ I have never shared a room before

I am:

☐ an early bird　☐ a late riser

PENN STATE UNIVERSITY HOUSING OFFICE: ROOMMATE AGREEMENT

When I am asleep it is okay for my roommate to:

☐ have music on   ☐ have the TV on   ☐ use a desk light   ☐ have guests over

☐ talk on the phone   ☐ use the computer   ☐ have the overhead light on

Is this true for both morning and night?

☐ yes ☐ no

I prefer living in a room that is:

☐ quiet   ☐ has some noise   ☐ has constant noise

I prefer to study:

☐ in my room   ☐ in the library   ☐ other

☐ in the morning   ☐ in the afternoon   ☐ in the evening   ☐ in the late evening

When studying in my room, I prefer:

☐ complete quiet   ☐ low music   ☐ loud music   ☐ television

I prefer our room be kept:

☐ neat   ☐ in between   ☐ messy   ☐ no preference

Borrowing personal belongings is: (including computer)

☐ okay   ☐ not okay   ☐ depends   ☐ no preference

If the answer is "depends," please elaborate on desired conditions:

When it comes to privacy, I need:

☐ a lot   ☐ some   ☐ very little

Roommate name _____

☐ I have shared a room before   ☐ I have never shared a room before

PENN STATE UNIVERSITY HOUSING OFFICE: ROOMMATE AGREEMENT

I am: ☐ an early bird ☐ a late riser

When I am asleep it is okay for my roommate to:

☐ have music on ☐ have the TV on ☐ use a desk light ☐ have guests over

☐ talk on the phone ☐ use the computer ☐ have the overhead light on

Is this true for both morning and night?

☐ yes ☐ no

I prefer living in a room that is:

☐ quiet ☐ has some noise ☐ has constant noise

I prefer to study:

☐ in my room ☐ in the library ☐ other

☐ in the morning ☐ in the afternoon ☐ in the evening ☐ in the late evening

When studying in my room, I prefer:

☐ complete quiet ☐ low music ☐ loud music ☐ television

I prefer our room be kept:

☐ neat ☐ in between ☐ messy ☐ no preference

Borrowing personal belongings is: (including computer)

☐ okay ☐ not okay ☐ depends ☐ no preference

If your answer is "depends," please elaborate on desired conditions:

When it comes to privacy, I need:

☐ a lot ☐ some ☐ very little

PENN STATE UNIVERSITY HOUSING OFFICE: ROOMMATE AGREEMENT

(To be agreed upon by all roommates)

We will clean our room ... Cleaning products purchased ... Have designated cleaning tasks?

☐ daily   ☐ weekly   ☐ separately   ☐ jointly   ☐ yes   ☐ no

☐ monthly   ☐ as needed

Name _____

Arrangements for overnight guests should be made:

_____ days / _____ weeks in advance

When it comes to having overnight guests/friends:

☐ I would mind male guests   ☐ I would not mind male guests

☐ I would mind female guests   ☐ I would not mind female guests

Significant other

☐ I would mind   ☐ I would not mind

My roommate's guests using my bed to sit on or sleep in is:

☐ okay   ☐ not okay

Overnight guests are allowed (to be agreed upon):

☐ every weekend   ☐ every other weekend   ☐ once a month

☐ 2-3 times per semester

I usually go to bed:

☐ before 11 p.m.   ☐ between 11 p.m. & midnight

☐ between midnight and 1 a.m.   ☐ after 1 a.m.

PENN STATE UNIVERSITY HOUSING OFFICE: ROOMMATE AGREEMENT

I expect to receive phone calls after 11 p.m. or before 8 a.m:

☐ frequently   ☐ sometimes   ☐ never

I have concerns about receiving calls after 11 p.m. or before 8 a.m:

☐ yes   ☐ no

I prefer the room temperature to be:

☐ cool   ☐ warm   ☐ very warm

I prefer the windows to be:

☐ open   ☐ closed   ☐ depends on the weather   ☐ no preference

If the answer is "depends," please elaborate on desired conditions:

Can your roommate eat your food? ☐ yes ☐ no

Do you prefer an alcohol-free room?

☐ yes   ☐ no   ☐ no preference

Changing Patterns of Roommate Conflict Fueled by the Net

by Bill Warters

From: Conflict Management in Higher Education Report
Vol. 6, Number 1, November 2005
Campus Conflict Resolution Resources Project
Department of Communication
Wayne State University
585 Manoogian Hall, Detroit, MI 48201

An October 16, 2005 article in The (Baltimore) Sun titled "Uneasy relations: Blogs, Web sites and instant messaging offer more ways for college roommates to be dysfunctional" explored roommate-conflict patterns among our "net-gen" students.

The article cites a 2004 survey of 31,000 freshmen across the country conducted by the Higher Education Research Institute at the University of California Los Angeles. The survey found that 29 percent of freshman reported having problems with their roommates. Female students were slightly more likely than their male counterparts to have conflicts.

While learning to live with a roommate has long been one of the challenges of college, housing officials cited in the article indicate that now 80 to 90 percent of incoming freshmen have never shared a room before they get to campus. This compares to about 50 percent a generation ago.

These students also tend to have active parents whose involvement may extend into their college lives, and these students are used to having many of their problems solved for them.

Of particular interest is the finding that students are used to talking online and in text messages, and are often more comfortable communicating complaints (directly or indirectly) via online methods instead of by face-to-face communication. Students in the same room will often use instant messaging to communicate rather than turning and talking to each other. They may complain about their roommate on a blog or in a chat session or by using text messaging on phones, creating new ways for students to become alienated from each other.

In related research not reported in The Sun article, the

2004 Higher Education Research Institute's "The American Freshman" report noted an increasing polarization in student political orientations. A record number of students label themselves as politically "far left" (3.4 percent) and "far right" (2.2 percent). While still small, these numbers indicate a significant increase over time in the proportion of students who define themselves at the political extremes. Also, identification as either "liberal" (26.1 percent) or "conservative" (21.9 percent) increased from 2003 to 2004. The political shift away from the center, concurrent with the presidential election year, is the largest one-year shift in the thirty-five years that the item has been measured. This polarization can lead to significant tensions on campus.

Certainly these results suggest a continued need for campus mediation work. And while the Internet may be contributing to communication problems, it can also be employed to support constructive conflict resolution. Recent reports of high schools using instant messaging "help lines" to resolve student conflicts and colleges that are using Web-based mediation-intake forms are a few examples of where we may be headed in the future.

As channels of communication increase, so do the opportunities for conflict. Hopefully the "digital-native" mediators among us will help lead the way by developing new forms of conflict management that suit the needs and styles of today's students. I'll certainly be watching with interest.

Ten Crucial Tips for Getting Along with Your Roommate

Department of University Housing

The University of Georgia
www.uga.edu/housing

1. Get to know each other.

You're going to be spending much time with your roommate and he or she is your first opportunity to make a new friend at UGA. Take the time to ask and answer questions — about family, hobbies, academic interests, etc. Who is this person? Some questions you can ask:

- My nickname is…

- My birthday is…

- The kinds of grades I want to earn this semester are…

- The kinds of food I like to eat are…

- The things I do for fun are…

- What I like to do for exercise is…

- Some things I spend my money on…

- Some things about my family are…

- Why I came to UGA is….

- My major is (or may be)…

- Some things about my hometown/high school are…

2. Communicate.

Open and honest communication is key in building a positive and successful relationship. Take some time and talk to each other and let your roommate know what is important to you. Talk about how you would like for the two of you to communicate with each other and how you talk to others when there is a problem or conflict. Living together can be stressful and knowing how the other person operates means that you can resolve conflicts before they grow too large. Healthy relationships take work. Some issues you may wish to discuss include:

- The way I feel about loaning things is…

- The way I would like to decorate our room is…

- If something I do upsets you, you would…

- When I am unhappy or mad, I…

3. Be open and friendly.

Both of you may be anxious and concerned about living with another person. Your roommate may be experiencing the same issues and concerns that you are and may be under the same pressures. Talk to each other about what is important to you and things that may affect your relationship as roommates.

- The way I feel about dating is…

- My favorite movie is…

- My favorite food is…

• My ideal vacation would be to go to…

4. Define "neat."

Whether you're a neat freak or a slob, you have someone else's feelings to consider. With a little give and take, you can each adjust accordingly and make your environment comfortable. You need to make sure that you both (1) agree to how you are going to keep the room, and (2) what you are going to do if one of you is not living up to your agreement.

5. Discuss visitation hours.

Talk about when it is okay and when it is not okay to have visitors in the room. Also discuss how often you both plan to have people over. Do you want your room to be a social center or a refuge from the crowds? How about opposite-gender guests? When are they allowed in the room? Do you think you might have overnight guests? What are the rules for them?

• I would like to avoid having guests over at these times…

• If I feel that a visitor(s) overstays his/her welcome, we would handle it by…

• The way I feel about your friends using my things is…

• The way I feel about having people in the room when I am trying to study is…

• The way I feel about getting dressed with members of the opposite sex in the room is…

• The way I feel about getting dressed with members of the same sex in the room is…

6. Find an activity you can share.

Nothing compares to having something in common to care and talk about. Do you both plan to go to Ramsey Student Center? Maybe you can be workout partners. Perhaps you both enjoy a particular type of film, music, art, or hobby. Do you plan to join any clubs or student organizations? While you will not be spending all your time with your roommate, it does not mean you can't do some things together.

7. What about study times and habits?

Talk about how you prepare for classes and tests. Do you study in the room or in another place such as the library, a study room, or the student learning center? If you plan on doing most of your work in your room, talk about scheduling times so that you both can fully use the room and not conflict with each other's activities. Let your roommate know when you have a big test or assignment coming up so that he or she can give you space and quiet time.

8. Give each other space.

Togetherness is great but too much of a good thing is sometimes not so great. You and your roommate need time alone or with other friends. If that is not happening naturally, talk about it.

9. Are you okay with sharing?

Just because you share a room, it does not mean you may want to share other things, even if you suddenly have twice the wardrobe. Talk about what you want to share and what you want to keep for yourself. Can you share a TV? Phone? Refrigerator? What about clothes, CDs, appliances, food, etc.? Setting these boundaries early can avoid later conflicts.

- Sharing a computer?

- Sharing a television

- Sharing a stereo?

- Sharing a game box (Xbox, PlayStation, etc.)

10. Pet peeves and personal habits.

What are your big pet peeves? What really bothers you? How do you deal with conflict? Do you yell, get quiet, or nurse a grudge? You have the chance to talk in advance before you establish a relationship with this person — use it.

- The way I feel about loaning things is...

- The way I react when I am stressed out is...

- When I am depressed I...

- Something that cheers me up when I am down is...

- I usually let people know I am angry by...

- I become easily annoyed by....

What to Expect When You Arrive at College

Getting acquainted with your surroundings and adjusting to college life

By Megan O'Leary-Buda
From: **www.collegeview.com**

Moving to college and adjusting to college life can be an overwhelming experience, especially if you have not been acquainted with the campus before.

For those of you who are living on campus, after moving all of your belongings into the residence hall, you should try to make a personal tour of the campus. This will make for an easier transition on the first day of class. Be sure to make a list of places to find. For instance, you will want to know where and when you can eat at the various places on campus.

If applicable, find out where you need to go to put money on your ID card. Many universities offer a plan to place money on the student ID card; you can spend that money on laundry, local food places, and even the bookstore. You should also go to the bookstore to find out what books you will need for your classes.

During move-in weekend, every student is in the same predicament. They are trying to adjust to college dorm life just like you are. They do not have all of the answers, but they do have some. Compare notes with them. They may have already found the information that you were looking for.

It is also encouraged to find a new person on the floor and find ways to get to know them better. You might even want to go together to find various offices and what each office offers to the students at your university.

The best advice is to ask as many questions as you have. There is never a stupid question. If you feel uncomfortable asking questions in the offices, find an upperclassman to help you. They have been in your shoes before and usually are willing to help and give a college freshman advice.

Megan O'Leary-Buda holds a master's degree in higher education administration from The University of Akron. She works at Quinnipiac University as a residence-hall director for off-campus properties, a position that allows her to create new programs for first-year transfer students, sophomores, and juniors. She also supervises resident assistants living in the neighborhoods surrounding the campus.

What to Bring to College – Your Dorm Room Checklist

Helping you pack the essential supplies for your first year of college dorm life.

By Megan O'Leary-Buda
From: **www.collegeview.com**

Before running out to the nearest store to purchase items for your dorm room, it is a great idea to check out your college's Web site (more specifically their Office of Residence Life page).

Frequently, there will be a list of items that are not permitted on campus, sometimes including air conditioners, space heaters, pets, toasters, etc.

Also, be sure to contact your college roommate to decide who is bringing what items from your dorm-room checklist. This lowers the possibility of a duplicate supply of items that may not fit in the small dorm room storage space.

Here's a college dorm-room checklist of essential items that you will want to bring:

- Alarm clock

- Bed linens/towels

- Carpet/throw rug

- Chair/bean bag

- Clothes-drying rack

- Compact refrigerator

- Computer

- Cup/mug/glass/plate/bowl/silverware

- Dish soap

- Fan

- Fish

- Handi-Tak to hang posters

- Hangers

- Iron

- Laundry bag

- Laundry detergent

- Medicine

- Microwave (one cubic foot)

- Plants (real or fake)

- Radio/stereo

- Rolls of quarters for laundry

- School supplies

- Sewing kit

- Shower caddy

- Telephone

- Toiletry items/soap dish

- TV/VCR/DVD player

Megan O'Leary-Buda holds a master's degree in higher education administration from The University of Akron. She works at Quinnipiac University as a residence-hall director for off-campus properties, a position that allows her to create new programs for first-year transfer students, sophomores, and juniors. She also supervises resident assistants living in the neighborhoods surrounding the campus.

Appendix B: Depression in College

From **www.mentalhealthamerica.net** (Mental Health America)

Sometimes the multitude of life's changes that occur during your college years can trigger serious depression. At this vulnerable time, the smartest thing you can do for yourself is to seek help. If your feelings of constant stress and sadness go on for weeks or months, you may be experiencing more than just difficulty adjusting to life's changes. Seek assistance from a doctor or mental-health professional, the university counseling service, or the student-health center. While in treatment, there are a number of steps you can take to help you cope on your way to recovery.

Carefully plan your day. Every day, list the work you need to do in order of importance. Setting priorities can give you a sense of control over what you must do and a sense that you can do it.

Plan your work and sleep schedules. Too many students defer doing important class work until nighttime, work through much of the night, and start every day feeling exhausted. Constant fatigue can be a critical trigger for depression. Seven or eight hours of sleep a night is crucial to your well-being.

Participate in an extracurricular activity. Sports, theater, fraternities and sororities, the student newspaper — whatever interests you — can bring opportunities to meet people interested in the same things you are, and these activities provide a welcomed change from class work.

Seek support from other people. This may be a roommate or a friend from class. Friendships can help make a strange place feel more friendly and comfortable. Sharing your emotions reduces isolation and helps you realize that you are not alone.

Try relaxation methods. These include meditation, deep breathing, warm baths, long walks, exercise — whatever you enjoy that lessens your feelings of stress and discomfort.

Take time for yourself every day. Make special time for yourself — even if it is only for 15 minutes a day. Focusing on yourself can be energizing and gives you a feeling of purpose and control over your life.

Work toward recovery. The most important step in combating depression and reclaiming your college experience is to seek treatment. Your physician should communicate to you that remission of symptoms should be your goal and work with you to determine whether psychological counseling, medication, or a combination of both treatments is needed.

For more information: For help in paying for your medications or finding treatment, support groups, medication information, your local Mental Health America affiliate, and other mental-health-related services in your community, please see Frequently Asked Questions at **www.mentalhealthamerica.net**. If you or someone you know is in crisis now, seek help immediately. Call 1-800-273-TALK (8255) to reach a 24-hour crisis center or dial 911 for immediate assistance.

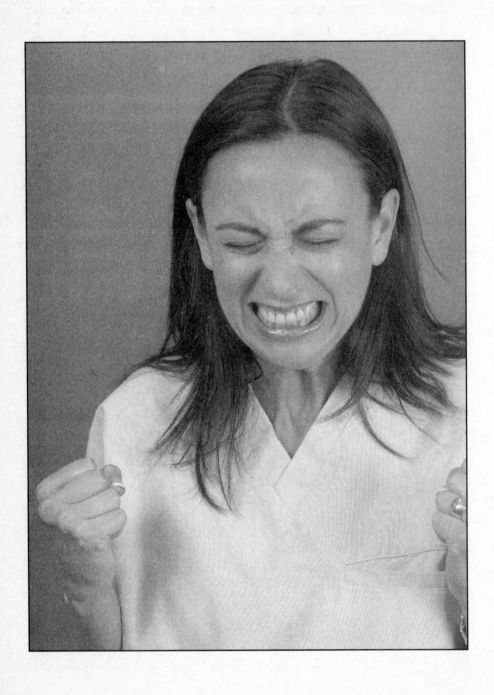

Appendix C:
Q&A with Author and Residence Life Area Coordinators

CASE STUDY: CAROLYNN S. NATH

Area Coordinator

Department of Housing and Residence Life

University of Central Florida

Q: What are some of the most common conflicts between roommates?

<u>Lack of Communication:</u> Students will often resort to writing notes back and forth, avoiding communication. Seek out a resident assistant or other staff member to help facilitate confrontation and communication. Common communication conflicts arise from the following:

- Communicating through virtual sources (Facebook, blogs, IM, and so on).

- Communicating though written form (dry-erase boards, Post-it notes, labeling with marker/tape).

- Communication through third parties (other roommates, guests, mutual friends).

- Unwillingness to confront the other person on her own and ignoring the situation(s).

CASE STUDY: CAROLYNN S. NATH

- Not seeing each other enough. People often think their roommate is going to be their best friend or they moved in with a best friend from high school. Living with someone often changes the dynamic of a friendship. If you can tolerate living with each other, realize friends come and go, then get involved on campus and make new friends.

Cleanliness: Make a schedule and revise it each semester. Include the following tasks:

- Trash (kitchen, bathroom)

- Laundry

- Bathrooms (toiletries, clean tub/shower, sink, mirrors, floors)

- Refrigerator/pantry (old food, stale food, stinky food)

- Cleaning

Thermostat

- Climate differences (for example, a student from a warmer climate or different hemisphere may want a warmer climate; students from cooler regions may like it cooler or want windows open in the spring or winter)

Guests

- Roommates are not informed guests are coming by or it is not communicated that certain people are unwanted visitors

- Guests stay for an extended period of time

- Guests are disrespectful and use a roommate's belongings when she is not home

- Guests violate housing policies, which may put the entire unit at risk

Well-Being Concerns:

- Mental health
- Eating disorders

CASE STUDY: CAROLYNN S. NATH

- Alcohol and or drug abuse
- Violent, abusive, or controlling relationships
- Family problems

Q: When students come to you for assistance, what are some of the problems with which they need help?

Communicating issues and handling the issue on their own

Students often have not lived with another individual in this type of environment, where they do not have a parent or guardian deciding a solution for them. As a result, students often have a difficult time understanding how to approach the issue. They may not have the confidence to speak with the roommates face to face and need the support of staff.

Q: What procedure is in place to help roommates resolve conflicts?

Staff members, often called resident assistants, are in resident halls across the nation. These staff members have extensive training to mediate communication. At the University of Central Florida, we also have graduate student staff and master's-level professional staff to guide and facilitate these conversations between roommates. Universities also have offices or departments that work specifically with students in need of mediation or a neutral party to aid in communication or personal conflicts.

Q: Do you provide students with guidelines for conflict resolution?

There are general guidelines for all residence halls, called community-living guides or residence-hall rules. At UCF, community-living guides can be found online on the housing Web page. At move-in, each student receives a copy and additional copies are at the residence-hall duty stations. Most universities provide a booklet of residence-hall rules and guidelines upon move-in to a campus facility. However, students often do not take the time to read them, which is why most students get fines or conduct meetings within the first month of moving in. These rules and policies are also reviewed at the first mandatory floor meeting. This is a great opportunity for you to get to know other residents on your floor or building and to ask questions about the rules and policies. Within these booklets of rules and policies are suggestions on how to handle a roommate conflict or how to approach a living situation and form a roommate contract where all roommates agree to the contents.

CASE STUDY: CAROLYNN S. NATH

Q: What advice can you give students before completing the placement forms when initially requesting housing?

- Think about how you live now, and subtract any family member who cleans up after you or tells you to clean your living space, do the dishes, and so on. When you think about how you live without that support, that is how you will live. Do not let your guardians choose your housing, because they will choose how they take care of you and not how you would live without them. This is part of the college process — welcome to the real world. People are not going to always hold your hand, and you are going to be held accountable for your own decisions and actions.

- Do your homework and get involved early. Think about living in a learning community or themed housing. This is a great way to get involved and gain new friends from day one. Ask yourself these questions: Do you like to stay fit? Look for a wellness or fitness community. Are you coming from out of state? You will have something in common with other folks looking to explore your new city. Are you focused on academics? Look for something that will support your study habits or see if your classes may be in your own residence hall. Do you like athletics? See if your residence hall is close to the intramural or athletic fields. These things will help you be selective and give you a better idea when choosing a residence hall.

Q: What advice can you give students in preparation for being and having a college roommate?

- Do not judge a book by its cover. Students and guardians often search on Internet sites (Facebook, MySpace, and others) to get a sense of who their roommate is. Having a roommate is about getting to know a person and giving him opportunities to explain himself. This is also why housing programs have roommate contracts so you can discuss living conditions and preferences. It is important to trust the system and see how you will live together rather than creating your own perception from stereotypes or other generalizations that you see on Internet sites.

- Determine before you arrive who is going to bring what items. There is nothing worse than moving in double items. I would suggest waiting until you move in to get many of your items, because measurements are also different in most rooms, bathrooms, and kitchen areas. This is also leaves you with fewer items to pack and move in.

CASE STUDY: CAROLYNN S. NATH

- Go green. Think about buying green items: sheets, towels, cleaning products, and so on. Shop at The Goodwill or thrift stores. Most items are gently used and were donated from former college students (if you are moving to a "college town") or check out free local items at **Craigslist.com**. See other green resources and ideas for college resident halls at:

www.thegreenguide.com/doc/121/dorm.

Carolynn S. Nath received her B.A. from the University of South Florida, her M.S. from Indiana University-Bloomington, and is working on an additional degree at the University of Central Florida. She has researched and presented at regional and national conferences on the following topics: social justice, safety and security, diversity education, sustainability and the collegiate environment, communication, and program and leadership development, as well as other issues facing students and staff at institutions of higher education. She is actively involved with the following national organizations: American College Personnel Association, National Association of Student Personnel Administrators, Association for Student Judicial Affairs, and the Association for College and University Housing Officers-International.

CASE STUDY: DAPHNE WELLS, M.ED

Residence Coordinator

The Florida State University

133 Wildwood Drive, Tallahassee, FL 32306

Dwells2@admin.fsu.edu

850-645-08525

Q: What are some of the most common conflicts b etween roommates?

Most students living in my hall have never had to share their space with anyone before. They come from homes where they have their own room and, as such, they have a hard time adjusting to living with someone else in a relatively small space. Thus, the most common conflict I deal with is the lack of respect for one's personal space. These conflicts range from being too loud (laughter, typing on their laptop, music, TV, cell phone ring tone etc.) to not appropriately sharing space in the refrigerator (two-liter sodas verses the single bottle of water). The most common problem is the early riser verses the night owl. I deal with a lot of students who "can't take another day" of their roommate's 1:30 a.m. costume change to go out on the town when they have to be up at 7 a.m. to get ready for class at 8 a.m. The same is true for the night owl who thinks it "ridiculously unreasonable" to have to tiptoe around the room because their roommate is in bed by 9 p.m. nother common conflict I deal with is guests. In particular, with my female residents it is their roommates' boyfriends. I have had many students come to me to express, their discomfort in having a male guest in their room. Most of the times it is as simple as having a guy (not related to you) in your personal space, but sometimes it is the heavy make-out sessions and occasional sexual rendezvous that really make the roommate uncomfortable.

Q: When students come to you for assistance, what are some of the problems with which they need help?

The students in my hall have a hard time confronting their roommates about the issues they are having with them. They do not want to cause any tension in the room so they come to me with their concerns about their roommates and want me to fix them. As you can imagine, that does not work. Other things students come to me with is how to help their roommates. I had a student contact me because her roommate cried hysterically every night and constantly made comments along the lines of "I want to die" and "I just don't want to do this anymore."

CASE STUDY: DAPHNE WELLS, M.ED

The student was concerned for her roommate and wanted to know what she (or I) could do to help. Along the same lines, I have had roommates come to me for assistance in relocating to another room because of the mental health of their roommates. I had to relocate one student because she didn't want to be "responsible" for her roommate should she follow through on her suicidal thoughts.

Q: What procedure is in place to help roommates resolve conflicts?

At my institution, we have roommate and suite-mate agreements that we have every resident complete with their RA. These are in place, ideally, to prevent any conflicts from arising between residents as the document forces the students to talk about their expectations. In addition to the agreements, we have the RA who is there to help the students talk through their differences and to mediate conflicts. During mediation, we meet with the students in a neutral location and give each roommate the opportunity to share his or her side of the story. Once both parties have said what they need to say, the RA works with the students to come to some resolution. If the RA is not successful (in that the issues persist) then the students meet with me to see what else can be done. Depending on the type of conflict, a student can either be removed from his/her room, the building, or from campus housing.

Q: Do you provide guidelines for conflict resolution?

Yes, we do. Our assistant director for Resident Life is in charge of training.

Q: What advice can you give students before completing the placement forms when initially requesting housing?

Do not bring your room to the residence halls! The number of students who bring so much stuff with them to college is ridiculous. So, that would be the first thing. Also, I would encourage them to read the fine print. We have policies that must be followed in the halls and if you break them, you will be held accountable. I hate when students act "surprised" that they cannot have candles in their rooms. Get to know your RA and hall director. They can be a great resource for the student. Get involved in hall government and let your voice be heard. Participate in the hall programs as they provide a great way to interact with others in the hall and often have valuable information for students.

CASE STUDY: DAPHNE WELLS, M.ED

Q: What advice can you give students in preparation for being and having a college roommate?

Many of my students have never shared a room before, so I would advise them to be open-minded and come expecting a totally new experience. Take the time to get to know your roommate and set up expectations early and revisit them throughout the year. They should learn how to share (within reason) as they will have a small area in which to live. Decorate the room together; it will give an opportunity to bond and allow the two to take ownership of their space. Commit to looking out for each other, travel together for safety, and lock the door when you leave. Don't allow people in the room by themselves when your roommate is not there.

Daphne Wells is a 2006 graduate of the Higher Education and Student Affairs Administration program at the University of Vermont and serves as Residence Coordinator of DeGraff Hall at the Florida State University. Daphne was introduced to the field of student affairs through the Minority Undergraduate Fellowship Program (Now known as the NASPA Undergraduate Fellowship Program) at the California State University-Chico, where she received her bachelors degree in sociology. A native of Sacramento, California, Daphne is enjoying the laid-back atmosphere of Tallahassee, Florida, and is looking forward to starting a doctoral program in the near future.

CASE STUDY: AYESHA RIZVI MIAN

Residence Life Coordinator

Department of Housing and Residence Education

University of Florida

18001001 Rawlings Hall

Gainesville, FL 32612

ayesharm@ufl.edu

Q: What are some of the most common conflicts between roommates?

- No. 1 — Privacy/guests and visitation/significant-others' visits or spending the night/having sex

- Cleanliness of the room/laundry on floor

- Personal hygiene

- Personal schedule/sleep schedules

- Inability to study in their room

- Roommate who is homosexual or an international student. Lately, I have seen little of this issue coming up but, in the past, it has been a bigger issue. Surprisingly, the complaint is commonly initiated by a parent.

Q: When students come to you for assistance, what are some of the problems with which they need help?

Roommate conflicts usually begin three to four weeks after students move in. The initial "honeymoon" phase is over and now they have really been able to get a feel for how the other person lives and what things are not compatible. More often than not, the students just want someone else to intervene and try to solve the problem. We encourage staff to move them in the direction of trying to open up lines of communication and truly express to each other what the problems are.

Sometimes they are so angry with the roommate they do not want to talk to them. Other times they are intimidated by an aggressive roommate. In some cases, the complainer will make an assumption that the roommate is doing things on purpose or that they are trying to annoy the complaining roommate enough to make them leave — a strategy designed to get them a room to themselves.

CASE STUDY: AYESHA RIZVI MIAN

This may be true in 25 percent of the cases, but in many cases, the other roommate does not even know that things are bothering the complainer.

Recently, many students come to college with pre-existing psychological issues that are aggravated in college when they are away from the comfort of their homes and do not have regularly monitored intake of medication or counseling that they may have received there.

Many do automatically compromise and talk about their issues. A majority of students manage to coexist just fine and often become good friends. In a small number of cases, there are significant differences, such as personal choice, tastes, and personality.

Q: What procedure is in place to help roommates resolve conflicts?

Our first step is to ask the student what they have done to communicate their concerns to their roommate. They are often hesitant to do this and do not want to be seen as "the bad guy." Students have become more hesitant when asked to confront a peer. It feels socially awkward to them, almost as though it is inappropriate. They are comfortable sending their friend an e-mail or a Facebook message instead of a face-to-face talk. Because students do not seem comfortable with direct communication, they are more unlikely to resolve issues on their own and frequently expect staff and family to intervene.

To be honest, the first I hear about a conflict between roommates is usually from the parent of one of the residents. Parental involvement is extremely high and, in many cases, I believe students are so used to parents fixing their problems for them that they prefer to call home, vent to a parent, and ask them to take care of it. From the parents' perspective, they hear about the news, get upset, and decide to initiate contact with staff in an effort to ease the problem, thereby fixing things for them. This assistance only serves as a handicap for students who have convinced themselves that someone else should be the one rectifying such differences.

If roommate interaction is not an ideal situation, then RAs step in to talk to each student. They help them understand the other's perspective and try to reach a compromise. I ask my staff that the compromise and mediation conversation do involve the students sitting face to face. This greatly helps open lines of communication. The agreement is documented in the form of a roommate contract or agreement — often a document housing staff use at the beginning of the year with all students.

CASE STUDY: AYESHA RIZVI MIAN

Any older versions are discarded because they are done upon the first few days of moving in together when. everyone is being nice to each other and they do not take the document seriously. Students are asked to hold each other responsible. If this fails, they move on to the RA's supervisor. Typically, that would be someone like me who tries some of the same techniques and, if all else fails, we go the route of switching their room if space permits the parent of one of the residents. Parental involvement is extremely high and, in many cases, I believe students are so used to parents fixing their problems for them that they prefer to call home, vent to a parent, and ask them to take care of it. From the parents' perspective, they hear about the news, get upset, and decide to initiate contact with staff in an effort to ease the problem, thereby fixing things for them. This assistance only serves as a handicap for students who have convinced themselves that someone else should be the one rectifying such differences.

If roommate interaction is not an ideal situation, then RAs step in to talk to each student. They help them understand the other's perspective and try to reach a compromise. I ask my staff that the compromise and mediation conversation do involve the students sitting face to face. This greatly helps open lines of communication. The agreement is documented in the form of a roommate contract or agreement — often a document housing staff use at the beginning of the year with all students. Any older versions are discarded because they are done upon the first few days of moving in together when everyone is being nice to each other and they do not take the document seriously. Students are asked to hold each other responsible. If this fails, they move on to the RA's supervisor. Typically, that would be someone like me who tries some of the same techniques and, if all else fails, we go the route of switching their room if space permits.

Q: Do you provide guidelines for conflict resolution?

There are really no guidelines except staff training and a discussion about the steps previously mentioned. Many schools do use a roommate agreement of some sort that they read and sign to document that a general agreement about life styles and habits has been reached. If there are issues, the roommate contract is pulled out to review what choices the roommates had decided on.

Q: What advice can you give students before completing the placement forms when initially requesting housing?

CASE STUDY: AYESHA RIZVI MIAN

The on-campus housing experience is amazing. I endorse it wholeheartedly. I came to the United States as an international student who knew no one here. My roommate had three different roommates in the fall semester, all of whom moved because of disciplinary or roommate-conflict reasons. She was nervous when I walked in during the spring semester. She had been hurt by some pretty difficult roommates and was nervous and drained at the thought of yet another one. But we somehow, as they say, "clicked" and have been great friends since. Many people are hesitant about living on campus because of small living quarters, privacy issues, public space (bathrooms and community kitchens/ lounges) and, most frequently, the rules students are asked to follow in residence halls.

I would advise students and their parents that they need to come into the college communal-living environment with an open mind. Conflicts will happen — they are inevitable. They happen between siblings, spouses, and friends all the time, all over the world and have for centuries. Some disagreements will happen. Students need to prepare to spend some time to get to know their roommate, be patient, and listen to each other, not make assumptions about each other, and try to solve problems themselves.

Parents are the biggest problem-creators since they get involved in even the smallest of the child's life experiences. They need to cut the cord and let their children discover what it is like to take care of things on their own.

Q: What advice can you give students in preparation for being and having a college roommate?

Be open-minded and do not come with preset expectations. Take things one day at a time.

Ayesha Rizvi Mian is a Residence Life Coordinator for the Department of Housing and Residence Education at the University of Florida. She received her bachelor's degree from the University of Arizona and master's in College Student Personnel Administration from Kansas State University. Her experience of working for residence-life programs at four different institutions, ranging from small, private colleges to large, public land-grant institutions, has helped provide her the chance to learn from some highly renowned systems and professionals in the field.

Appendix D: Case Studies

CASE STUDY: JOSH Z.

Graduate, private New England college

I got the name of my roommate over the summer, and we e-mailed each other about what to bring and our likes and dislikes. We seemed to have a lot in common. He told me he loved football. I had played in high school and am a huge Giants fan. I was going to be a percussion major, so I told him that I would be in the practice rooms after classes quite a bit. He also told me he was a big classical music fan, which I thought was cool. It never occurred to me to look him up on MySpace until a friend suggested it.

Well, I did look him up and I could not believe what he had posted. Not only was he into garage rock and goth, he made a point of trashing classical music. Then he trashed football and other sports. He made it a point to call sports fans "demented and stupid." It was not until I read the part of his blog that said music was not really a major and that anyone could play an instrument that I realized he was talking about me. He even went on to blog that he could not wait to meet his "jerk of a roommate who thinks I liked football."

I guess if anyone was demented and stupid, it is him. I e-mailed him and told him I had read what he posted on his blog. He never responded, which I took to mean he knew he was caught red-handed. Since I had applied early, I had enough time to request another roommate and things worked out fine. My advice to anyone who wants to know about their roommate is to first talk to them. Sometimes they will even tell you to read their MySpace page. It is not as though you are spying. Let us face it, if there is something someone does not want the public to know about them, the last place they should post it is online.

CASE STUDY: KAREN R.

Senior, Penn State University

What can I say? I had the worst roommate my first year. She came from a small town and it seems like she could not wait to drink herself into a stupor every weekend and sleep with every guy on campus. It only took her one week before she started bringing guys to our room. Most of them left but some stayed overnight. I had no  intention of sleeping in a room where they were having sex so I would stay with a friend I had known in high school who lived in another dorm.

At first I thought she would eventually get it out of her system and pay attention to classes and studying. She did manage to make it to classes, but complained about the amount of homework and how it left her less time to party. One weekend, while I was with friends at a movie, someone called me from a party and told me she had passed out. At first I said it was not my problem, but then I felt bad and worried that she would try to drive home when she woke up. So I had a friend drive me there and I helped get her in the car, where she puked. Not only did I have to drag her from the car to our room, but I had to clean up her puke.

That was about the last straw. I did not come to college to be a baby sitter. By December, things had not gotten any better. I wondered if she did not even realize her behavior was so disruptive, so I talked to her about it. She said she had been waiting years to get away from her family and her town to "finally have a life." It was clear that her behavior was not going to change overnight. I knew once her parents saw her grades, she would either have to clean up her act or leave.

I was right. During winter break, she e-mailed me to say that she was not coming back. It is funny that I ended up with a new roommate who had experienced the same thing and had asked to be moved. We had some good stories to share and tried to outdo each other. But my story of having to clean up puke in my own car was the best. We both agreed on that.

CASE STUDY: JESSICA O.

Graduate, University of Pennsylvania

I have so many bad roommate stories but one of the best was this woman I roomed with in my freshman year (of all years!) who had absolutely no problem walking around stark naked. Not just in our room, but down the hall to the shower, into the toilet stall, back down the hall, and even into the kitchen area. We were in a coed dorm too, so it is not like there were just a few girls around. Sometimes she would drape a small towel around her waist, but it barely covered what it was supposed to.

People stared and whispered, and she must have known they were talking about her. I kind of felt bad for her, but not so much because I just could not believe she had that kind of nerve. The thing was, and this is kind of mean, she was on the heavy side, which made it even more embarrassing. Or I should say, made me even more embarrassed for her because not only were people talking about her obsession with being naked, they were making fun of her body.

I put up with this for a few weeks until I came home from class one day and she was sitting — completely naked — on my quilt. I was totally grossed out and went crazy. I just kind of lost it and said, "If you want to make a fool of yourself and walk around like no one notices, that's fine, but I don't want your fat rear on any of my stuff."

Believe it or not, she seemed surprised . . . as if it had never occurred to her that her behavior was just weird. I apologized the next day but only for yelling at her. I made it clear that I was not comfortable with her nakedness and especially having her butt on my bed. I told her people talked about her, too. She just kind of shrugged and said one of the reasons she wanted to go to Penn was because it was a "progressive" university. Well, yeah, maybe by way of academics, but it is not a nudist camp. She had some other issues too, like depression and family problems, so being around her was a drag. I eventually moved off campus to live with some friends who preferred to keep their clothes on.

CASE STUDY: ASHLEIGH B.

Junior, private university
Philadelphia, Pennsylvania

I knew absolutely nothing about drugs or drug use when
I started here two years ago. I grew up nearby, but my
parents thought it was a good idea for me to live on
campus so I could become more independent. They
regretted that decision after the first semester.

I was going to be traveling abroad to study during my sophomore year, so I had
to maintain a certain grade-point average while a freshman. Needless to say, I
studied all the time but, since I lived near home, I went there on weekends. Little
did I know my roommate, Lisa, was doing and dealing drugs while I was away. I
saw the first signs of it when I found a plastic needle casing in the trash. At first I
thought she was diabetic. We did not spend time with each other outside the room
so I really did not know much about her personal life. I did not say anything but
started checking the bathroom trash can on Mondays. Sure enough, there was
another one. I took it out of the trash and put it in a plastic bag. I did not really have
a plan to do anything with it but just thought it was a good idea.

Along with that, our room was a disaster when I returned Sunday nights. I could tell
someone had been sleeping in my bed. I confronted Lisa and she said something
like, "Oh, yeah. My sister was here and there wasn't enough room in my bed, so she
slept in yours. You don't mind, do you?" I told her that I *did* mind and asked that no
one sleep in my bed and that she be more considerate and clean up on Sunday.

I started asking other students on my floor if they saw people coming and going
from my room. One guy told me he thought we had parties every weekend because
there was so much traffic. I confronted Lisa and she admitted to having a few
people over but said the other guy was exaggerating. The next weekend, I spied
on my own room. I came to campus with my older brother on Saturday night. We
stood at the end of the hall where we could see the door to my room, but anyone
coming out would have to go in the opposite direction to get to the elevator. I
could not believe it. There was a steady stream of people. They would stay a few
minutes and then leave and we could even see some of them stuffing something
in their pockets.

We went home and told my dad who immediately called campus police. Lisa
was busted that night and we found out my room had been raided. After that, my
parents insisted I move back home until it was time to go abroad. I moved back on
campus and into a single the following year.

CASE STUDY: KATHRYN F.

Student at the University of Massachusetts

We were friends from work and had a lot of fun together, so we thought being roommates would be a great idea. We found a two-bedroom apartment and moved in right before the beginning of my sophomore year. Her two Siamese cats, male and female, moved in, too.

Things were all right at first, but then she began to use drugs. I tried not to judge what she was doing, but I did not want any drugs or drug use in the apartment I was paying rent for. She went ahead and did it anyway behind closed doors.

Then she started to eat my food. I was taking a full load of classes and working as well, so I was in no position to buy food for both of us. She would try to be sneaky and steal a soda from the back of the six-pack thinking I would never catch on.

Halfway through the second semester, she took off . . . just got up and left without any notice but did not take the cats. I was left with no other choice but to feed (and pay for the food) and pick up after them. The worst part was that she had never had them fixed, so, of course, the female went into heat and it was a nightmare.

After a week or two of her being gone, I found out she stopped paying rent as well. After numerous calls (at least 30 before her dad finally returned one) to her and her parents, someone finally paid the back-due rent and came to pick up the cats. But because I had to cover a portion of her rent and had to move out before the lease expired, since I could not afford the rent on my own, I lost the security deposit. Because we had a joint lease, we were both responsible. If I had not forgone the security deposit, it would have appeared on my parents' credit report since they had been cosigners.

Thankfully, the lease ended and I came out alive, just minus $250, which can be a lot of money for a college student.

What I learned from this experience is to know someone well before you sign a lease with them, and read the fine print on your lease or any contract you sign. Your roommate may get up and leave, and you may not know that you are responsible for their half of the rent.

CASE STUDY: GARY F.

Graduate of Florida Institute of Technology

I went to a small school where the ratio of men to women was 20 to one, which made for an interesting environment. Some of the male students would go out of their way to be strange, as if that would be a selling point to the female students. So from the beginning, I wasn't that surprised to be matched with an odd roommate. I was surprised that I would be matched with a string of them over the next four years.

The first guy seemed really studious, polite, and well-adjusted. He brought his parents to the room and introduced them to me. My major was aeronautics and his was engineering. If there is a stereotype of an engineering student, he was it; he wore thick glasses and a white, short-sleeve shirt, that even had a plastic pocket protector. His folks took us both to dinner and he seemed like a well-mannered young man whose goal was to get good grades, please his parents, and get a job.

Do not let looks deceive you. For the first few weeks, all he did was study. Then his opposite personality kicked in. He started partying and staying out all night. He would sleep through classes — well into the afternoon and then yell at me for opening the shades at 3 p.m. He held parties in the hallways and was so loud and disruptive, he eventually got thrown out of the dorm. This was before the first semester even ended. He moved his stuff out and went to live off campus with friends. That was the end of Bad Roommate No. 1.

My next roommate was from Tennessee. He chewed tobacco and was obsessed with fire-brewed beer. He could explain in painful detail the step-by-step brewing process and which brands were better than others and why. For someone like me, who favored whichever beer was on tap, it was about as annoying as the tobacco chewing and spitting, which was fairly annoying, along with the giant wad constantly bulging from the side of his mouth. I am not even sure how he managed to get accepted. He lasted one semester and then dropped out. Probably to open up a brewery. End of roommate No. 2.

My next roommate was a martial arts fanatic and would practice his moves on anyone who innocently walked down the hall. He also had a hobby of disassembling the dorm furniture, which I believe was in violation of dorm policies. Maybe he was into feng shui, or maybe it was because the furniture had been taken apart, but he liked to sleep on the floor, surrounded by candles, which I believe was another violation. I did not wait for him to drop out. I moved to an off-campus apartment and spent the remaining years at FIT living happily by myself.

CASE STUDY: THE WORST COLLEGE ROOMMATE:
HOW I BECAME A RELUCTANT VOYEUR

The Sounds of Sex
By Fern Cohen
www.ferncohen.com
Published by **www.associatedcontent.com**
November 14, 2007

I have had my share of less-than-ideal roommates. God knows, college is difficult enough without coming home to a space the size of a closet that is stuffed with two beds, a fridge, hotplate, and tons of books and papers. If they gave out frequent-stayer points for the library, I certainly would have racked up enough credit to buy my own house off campus. I always seemed to get stuck with the homesick, boyfriend-missing wretch who decided to leave after a year to move home and commute, or who transferred to a campus closer to home. I began to think I was the one who drove them away. Nevertheless, each year I had a new personality to get used to. My freshman roommate went home every weekend, leaving me lonely at first, but grateful once I had a boyfriend. I dated a pre-med student for three years, so the peace and quiet of a roommate-free dorm room was great. The rest of the time, we went off to the library. Dating a pre-med student was definitely my salvation, since I doubt I would have been so studious if I had paired up with the dorm pothead.

I find it hard to pick out my worst experience. That freshman-year roommate who went home every weekend, made up for the weekend peace with endless phone calls every weekday evening to her best friend, mom, and boyfriend, during which she cried and counted the days when she would go home again. No surprise that she left after that year to attend the local college near her home. Enter the severe asthmatic my second year. She was nice, but the poor thing chose a school in the worst ragweed territory in New York. After many asthma attacks and sleepless nights spent pacing the floor, she too went home to live. The third year I got the loud snorer. "If you hear me snore during the night, just roll me over on my stomach," she told me. She was big; rolling her over would not have been easy. Besides, I didn't feel like repositioning a full-grown 19-year-old who woke me at three in the morning. I was afraid to approach her bed, lest I satisfy my temptation to smother her with a pillow, silencing her snores forever and putting me in a jail cell with an even worse roommate.

Senior year held promise. I found a roommate who was a late-night partier, but so was I. We were almost out of there and determined to have fun. By that time, I had broken off with the future doc and was manhunting myself.

CASE STUDY: THE WORST COLLEGE ROOMMATE: HOW I BECAME A RELUCTANT VOYEUR

She was a lot more active and brought guys back to have sex. But I didn't mind sleeping on the couch in our suite's sitting room a few nights a week. When we both signed on for student teaching the second semester of senior year, and had to wake up at 6:30 every morning, I figured the sex in our room would stop. Wrong. So I secured my place in the room and in bed by 10 every night, while she entertained her men friends out in the sitting room, a little miffed that I was already inside and in bed. Ha! Got you there.

Or so I thought until one night I awoke to loud moaning. Oh, no, I thought. The snorer cannot be back. But this was not snoring, and it was not coming from a female. I could not, would not believe that my nymphomaniac roommate was having sex in the next bed. When I brought up the subject the next day, she told me I was free to go elsewhere. Yeah, right. Try finding a new room, and a new roommate in March of your senior year. She was not embarrassed that I had heard. But wait — it gets worse. A few nights later, I heard whispering. "You can't stay all night in my bed; you have to leave and go to your own bed," I heard her telling her semi-steady sex partner (she had other "johns" too, but this one was pretty regular.) So this time I heard loud banging. This time they were standing against the door to our room, hence the banging. Oh, great, I said to myself. All through, she maintained her attitude. "So leave!" she would tell me. So, bleary-eyed, I would face my students, praying for May and graduation. Thankfully, time flew as it always does. I went my way, and my libidinous roommate went hers.

It is hard to believe that more than thirty years have passed. About five years ago, I received a message on my classmates.com profile from a guy who lived in my dorm during my senior year of college. I recognized the name and chuckled. We chatted by instant message. I reminded him of those hot, steamy sex sessions he had with my roommate, and to which I was an unwilling "entendeur" ("voyeur" comes from the French "one who sees." I was only "one who hears;" hence an "entendeur"). He was so embarrassed. My raunchy roomie had him convinced I was a deep sleeper and had not heard a thing. How stupid a 19-year-old can be when caught with his pants down in front of some lying vixen. "If I'd known you heard everything," he said. "I never would have banged her right in the room with you there." I tended to doubt that. I do not think it would have made a difference. He shot over a picture of a paunchy, balding middle-age man, his wife (not my college roommate), and two grown sons. I wondered if that woman could ever imagine that her hubbie honed his skills surreptitiously within earshot of an unwilling observer who just wanted a good night's sleep before honing her skills in the classroom the next day.

CASE STUDY: S. SMITH

Graduate of Syracuse University

Prior to my first day of college, I received notice that, due to larger than anticipated enrollment, I would share a converted public room with three other girls. Needless to say, I was apprehensive about the logistics. My nervousness was magnified when I decided to phone my three soon-to-be roommates to make introductions.

The first — a girl from Long Island — immediately asked me my race. The second, from Manhattan, never returned my call. The third — from a rural town with a population of less than 100 — sounded nervous but nice. As it turns out, the third one was the loose cannon.

We all checked in on the first day and got acclimated to our new surroundings. By day two, we were ready to engage the full-on college experience by starting up a drinking game. When we asked roomie No. 3 if she wanted to join in, she said that she had never drunk beer before but would be pleased if we let her watch. We all felt a little uncomfortable but said that was okay.

As we began to line up shot glasses and bottles of beer, she would pick up each and carefully examine it, holding it up to the light as if it were a jewel or a fossil. As we sat in a circle to begin our game, she asked if we could "bless" the game. We said "no." Next, as we began to play and each took a turn drinking, No. 3 would sort of scoot into the personal space of the designated drinker and carefully scrutinize every muscular movement of our faces and throats as we sucked down the contents of the shot glass.

As irony would have it, this uncomfortable experience taught us all that binge drinking was not that much fun. During our drinking game, Roomie No. 3 had made us feel a bit like aliens from another planet. Independently, we all came to the conclusion that getting drunk for the sake of getting drunk was, indeed, an unpleasant and bizarre sensation. But, irony is nothing without 180-degree turns and irony ends this story. Roomie No. 3 — that sweet, innocent, naïve girl from a farm in Middle America — became the most party-eager girl on our floor and remained that way through all of her years at college.

CASE STUDY: STEPHANIE K. CARTER-SMITH

Residence Life Coordinator
University of Florida Department of Housing and
Residence Education
stephaniec@housing.ufl.edu
Division of Student Affairs
SW 13th Street & Museum Road
PO Box 112100
Gainesville, FL 32611-2100
Phone: (352) 392-2161

Most conflicts result from the use of space in the room (for example one roommate has more items than the other and naturally thinks he or she can take up more room than the other person). Or there are differences with class/leisure-time schedules. One roommate enjoys going out every night, while the other is more focused on schoolwork and their schedules conflict like crazy. There are typically conflicts over cleanliness or lack thereof in residential spaces. You could not imagine some of the pure filthiness we as housing-staff members get to see when we walk into student spaces. Typically, when students come to us they need help communicating with each other. We live in an age where everything is done over the computer or sometimes through notes or letters, but no one wants to talk face to face to air out their grievances. When they find their way to my office, after they unsuccessfully handled the situation through their own means or through that of my other staff members, it is at a bad point. The roommates have typically cut off all verbal communication with each other, and sometimes they are maliciously doing things out of spite.

Our first line of communication is what we call at UF their Roommate Agreement Form. This is an opportunity for roommates to sit down at the beginning of the semester and talk about a few key points that could end up being disastrous if they got out of hand. Our staff promotes an environment of free thinking and sharing between the two or four students in the room to help curtail any future issues from arising. Sometimes this helps and other times it does not. If the Gator-to-Gator does not work, we have the residents speak with their RA to discuss the matter as a group. If that proves unsuccessful and no compromise can be met, the residents are referred to the graduate hall director of the area for another level of mediation. If that proves unsuccessful, the students are referred to the professional staff member in the building.

Typically, at this point, a decision will be reached. Either the two will stay together, or we will do our best to find space for one of the roommates elsewhere on campus. The key is coming to a resolution that will best benefit both individuals and allow them to focus on their education and not on their roommate conflict.

CASE STUDY: STEPHANIE K. CARTER-SMITH

The following is the information we list on our Housing Web site about roommate conflicts and conflict resolution:

Steps to resolving a roommate conflict

- **Step 1** — Complete the Gator-to-Gator Building Roommate Communications program with your roommate(s). See staff for info.

- **Step 2** — Speak to your roommate(s) directly. State issues neutrally. Relay feelings. Offer resolutions. Be prepared to listen. Be willing to compromise.

- **Step 3** — Ask staff assigned to your floor to intervene by meeting with all roommates involved. His/Her role is that of a neutral mediator as involved roommates resolve the problem.

- **Step 4** — Roommates meet with a graduate hall director, residence director, or residence-life coordinator who may serve as a mediator or arbitrator in resolving the conflict. Roommates may be asked to sign revised Roommate Expectations forms. If problems cannot be resolved, transfers may be arranged.

- **Step 5** — The assistant director of Housing for Residence Life may intervene in a conflict if roommates have been unable to resolve it at the other levels.

When filling out the questions on the housing forms **be honest.** If you do not like to study with music on do not put that you do. If you are a smoker and do not mind living with another smoker put that down. If you go to bed early and have ever since you were 12, do not somehow think now that you are in college that your schedule may change because it may not. The assignments staff at most universities do their best to match students as closely as they can from the answers/questionnaire results students provide. It is in your best interest to be honest so they can find the most compatible roommate for you to help your chances of having a successful year living on campus.

At the University of Florida during summer preview orientation sessions, the Department of Housing holds an educational session for parents and potential students. Our session covers everything from roommate relations, safety, and security — you name it — if it deals with living on campus, we touch on it in some way. During this time, we talk about keeping lines of communication open with your roommate and consulting with our staff if help is needed.

CASE STUDY: STEPHANIE K. CARTER-SMITH

When issues arise, discuss them as adults would. Air your grievances rationally and purposefully. Do not insult the other person and definitely do not call them names. When in doubt, remember you are never alone. We have competent student and professional staff in the area who can help you with your situation and come to an agreement in which all parties involved will find some benefit.

Stephanie K. Carter-Smith is a graduate of Florida State University and The University of Georgia. She received her master's degree in College Student Affairs Administration in 2002. She has worked in the field of student affairs since then. Carter-Smith worked for three years at Duke University (on-campus student housing), did a short stint in private student housing, and joined The University of Florida housing staff in January 2006. She supervises four graduate-hall directors and 27 RA staff members.

CASE STUDY: ALAN ACOSTA, RESIDENCE COORDINATOR

University Housing, The Florida State University
942 Learning Way • P.O. Box 3064174
Tallahassee, FL 32313-4174
Ph: (850) 644-3558 • Fax: (850) 645-7751
E-mail: aacosta@admin.fsu.edu

The most common roommate-related conflict I see is when one roommate behaves in a way that makes the other roommate uncomfortable. In these situations, there is often a serious policy violation, such as underage drinking or illegal drug use, which can make addressing the situation difficult.

Another common roommate issue is when one roommate disrupts the sleep of another on a consistent basis. Sometimes one roommate snores, making life uncomfortable for the other roommate. Sometimes one roommate feels they need to play music or leave the TV on to fall asleep and the other roommate needs absolute silence. Sometimes one roommate likes to have a light on and the other needs total darkness. One of the most common conflicts I have heard that is sleep-related is where Mary likes to stay up or stay out late, and when she comes back to the room she is loud and wakes up Jane, her roommate. I have also seen conflicts where the two roommates are on different sleeping patterns (one sleeps all day, the other all night). In most sleep-related conflicts, Jane wants to know how she can approach Mary and let her know that what she is doing is disrupting her sleep or try to find a way to change Mary's sleeping pattern.

CASE STUDY: ALAN ACOSTA, RESIDENCE COORDINATOR

Another conflict I see frequently is when one resident feels uncomfortable because of her roommate's guests. One I hear often is that Mary has her boyfriend/girlfriend over all the time and it makes Jane uncomfortable. Sometimes it is because Mary and her boyfriend/girlfriend are together all the time in the room or even having sex in the room, and it is a matter of Jane wanting some privacy. I had one conflict where Jane was tired of coming out of the shower in a towel and seeing Mary's boyfriend in the room. They will want to negotiate a guest policy with their roommate.

Students come to see me for a variety of problems. The most common reason residents come to see me is that they feel there is a problem with their current room assignment. Some of these problems include roommate conflicts, feeling like their room is too small, living in a room with too many people (such as a triple or quad room), they want to move to a "nicer" hall, or they want to move to a single room for more privacy. Sometimes residents see me if they want clarification about a housing policy, such as why they cannot have candles, why they got charged for damage in the room, and how they can get something in their room fixed.

Every so often students will come to me with an academic concern. I will point them in the direction of academic resources and ask them if there is anything we in housing can do to better their academic environment.

The way we address conflict depends on whether there is a policy violation taking place. If Jane tells me Mary is breaking a policy, such as underage drinking, I will tell Jane to document the situation using a behavior-report form. I will then sit down with Mary and talk to her about what I am hearing about her behavior, why it is a policy violation, and what some of the consequences are if she is documented violating the policy in the future. If the violation is more serious, such as Mary is selling drugs out of her room, I will have Jane contact campus police, and we will work together to address the situation from there.

If there is no policy violation taking place and it is just an issue between two roommates, I follow a four-step process:

1. If it has not happened already, I encourage Mary and Jane to talk to each other first. In many roommate conflicts, Mary is not even aware she is doing something that bothers Jane. Sometimes Mary just needs to be made aware that there is a problem, and it can be resolved quickly.

CASE STUDY: ALAN ACOSTA, RESIDENCE COORDINATOR

2. If that has not helped resolve the conflict, I will send the RA of that room to have a mediation session with Jane and Mary; if there are roommates living in the room who are not directly involved with the conflict, such as Rita, she will asked to attend the meeting also. The RA will go over the roommate agreement, a document we have the roommates of every room fill out with their RA at the beginning of the year, and address all issues that arise as they come up. The RA will then make sure Mary and Jane understand the agreement they have made and that they need to adhere to it to avoid future conflict. We always give the roommates a copy of the agreement and keep a copy on file in our office.

3. If problems persist, I will meet with the residents. I will look over the roommate agreement to see what they have talked about beforehand. When Jane and Mary come into my office, I will lay down a few ground rules: no name-calling; no interrupting each other; make sure they tell the truth; listen carefully; be polite and respectful when communicating; and be ready to compromise. If more than two residents are involved, I will also tell them to speak only for themselves. For example, if Mary is talking, she should not say to Jane, "Rita thinks you are awful." That may not be what Rita thinks. I then give each of them the opportunity to speak. I ask them to describe what they see as the problems in the room and ask them to tell me what they need to live comfortably in their space. I will take notes as they talk. Once all residents have made this clear, I will help identify how they can compromise with each other and feel comfortable in the room. I will inform them that they need to live by these newly established guidelines or they may be moved from the hall. After the meeting, I will send a letter to the residents detailing our meeting and re-emphasizing the compromises they agreed on.

4. If there are still conflicts, I will move Mary or Jane or both. At this point, one of them often wants to move, so I accommodate the request.

One piece of advice I would give is that a student should know what is important to him or her and rate that appropriately. If living in a "nicer" hall or a specific area on campus (some students like to live in certain halls because they are closer to their classes) is more important, they should rank that high. If a student wants to live with one roommate or by himself/herself, they should rank that high.

Visiting the campus to get an idea of the kind of residence halls the student will live in is also a great benefit. Understanding what the options are, what they look like, and where they are on campus will help a student clarify where he or she wants to live.

CASE STUDY: ALAN ACOSTA, RESIDENCE COORDINATOR

Finally, I would tell students to be open to the experience they have. Even if they do not get their top residence-hall choice or room preference, be ready to have fun and make the space their home. The first piece of advice I would give students preparing to live in a residence hall is not to judge a book by its cover. In the age of Facebook and MySpace, we have seen an increase in the number of concerns (mostly from parents) when a student decides he or she does not want to live with their roommate because of something they saw on their online profile, even before they have met their potential roommate.

If the housing department sends a student their roommate's contact information, they should talk together and get to know their potential roommate. Roommates should start talking about as many things as possible before moving in, such as what items they will bring, what items they can share, and what they will need to live successfully in the room.

I would also tell residents that if any problems arise, moving out of the room should be the last possible option. Try to talk it out with your roommate, get a housing-staff member involved, and do your best to try to make it work. Going through that process can resolve any conflicts in a more effective manner than moving out will.

Finally, be willing to compromise. Too many students come into the halls with a "my-way-or-the-highway" attitude, which makes things difficult for roommates and housing staff. Try to see things from the other person's point of view, and be ready to work with a roommate to set up the living space.

Alan Acosta began in housing as a resident assistant at the University of Florida (UF), where he worked from 2001 to 2004. After completing his BSBA in business management, Alan stayed at UF and worked as a graduate-hall director from 2004 to 2006 while completing his master's degree in education with a concentration in student personnel in higher education. During the summer of 2005, Alan worked as an Association of College and University Housing Officers-International (ACHUO-I) intern at The New School, a university in New York City. Alan has worked as a residence coordinator at Florida State University since July 2006.

CASE STUDY: KELLY R. DOEL

Area Coordinator
Housing Office
University of Central Florida
kdoel@mail.ucf.edu

The most common conflicts between roommates include issues with cleanliness, noise, overnight guests, and occasionally alcohol or drug use.

There are times students are reluctant to address issues with their roommates. During the first six weeks of the fall semester, or the "honeymoon" period, there is a higher sense of patience and understanding as roommates get to know each other. Little quirks, annoyances, and other issues are not always addressed but continue to occur. As mid-term exams approach, those things become bigger issues and students find it difficult to confront roommates, which is when they often meet with me. Issues brought to coordinators in my position often consist of the external ones such as cleanliness or overnight guests, but that leads to students needing help with the underlying issues of communication and confrontation skills.

We take an active approach by encouraging residents to complete a roommate agreement at the beginning of the fall semester. They are also encouraged to complete another agreement if a new roommate moves in at the beginning of the spring semester. This agreement allows roommates to discuss all aspects of living together, including who will clean what when, who will take out the garbage, during what hours visitors are allowed, at what temperature the air conditioning should be set, etc. This sparks communication right from the beginning and establishes a set of expectations agreed to by all. In many cases, this prevents conflict from occurring. If a conflict does arise during the semester, we hope residents will be able to work through it on their own by using their roommate agreement. If not, RAs are available to assist them in different ways. Sometimes a discussion with the RA is sufficient. A mediation, which RAs are trained to conduct, may be necessary as well. The RAs occasionally need assistance in conflict resolution, and graduate assistants or area coordinators complete a formal mediation with the roommates. It is then important for the residence-life staff to follow up with the roommates regularly to see if further assistance is needed. In the most extreme cases, the coordinator may refer the roommates to a formal mediation process with the dispute-resolutions office on their campus.

CASE STUDY: KELLY R. DOEL

Many residence-life programs educate residents on conflict resolution through programming initiatives, bulletin boards, community-living guides, and floor meetings at the beginning of each semester. It is important to note that each living environment differs, so educational techniques may be altered depending on the community. We focus on preparing students for living with roommates in our community-living guides, which can be found at **www.housing.ucf.edu/current/current.php**. Again, we take an active approach by providing information on roommate communication and setting expectations. We encourage residents to speak with their RA if they encounter a conflict.

We are finding that pairing roommates by preference results in no fewer roommate conflicts than random assigning. Some institutions no longer ask for general preferences. Students are able to say they prefer a specific person, but they do not fill out questionnaires that ask what time they go to bed, what type of music they listen to, and so on. For students who are given the opportunity to request a preferred type of roommate they are looking for at other institutions, I encourage them to be honest on the forms they are filling out. Parents may fill out the forms or watch their student fill them out. The responses can be skewed and not give a true picture of what type of person the student truly is. Honesty at the start will result in a better living environment later.

My advice to incoming residential students is to be open-minded to the idea of sharing space with people who may be different from themselves. Everyone brings their own set of values and experiences to college and that should be respected. To think you will be best friends with all of your roommates may not be realistic. I encourage students to communicate their expectations openly from the beginning and when an issue arises, address it immediately.

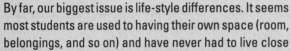

CASE STUDY: ANDREW J. DIES

Resident Director
Office of Housing & Residential Life
Temple University
Philadelphia, PA 19122

By far, our biggest issue is life-style differences. It seems most students are used to having their own space (room, belongings, and so on) and have never had to live close to another person. Whereas before they did not need to be cognizant of anyone else, living on campus in a residential setting forces them to be aware of another person's wants and needs. When they are not aware, roommate conflicts arise.

Students come to me when there is a conflict resulting from life-style differences. We do the best to pair up "like" roommates, but preferences listed on a housing application are not always accurate. Students come in and start to explore their newfound freedoms in college and do not always make the best choices. It seems those in the "Millennial Generation" are not comfortable in communicating their concerns to their roommates. On average, they would just as soon change rooms without dealing with the problem, or have their mom/dad/guardian contact the resident director to deal with the issue.

The first approach to resolving conflict is the Roommate Agreement, a preventative measure we take at the beginning of the year. This document prompts roommates to discuss things such as room cleanliness, sleeping and study habits, and so on. It is a great way to start the conversation about whether the roommates' life styles will mesh or clash.

As issues begin to arise during the year, we use the resident adviser (RA) staff to do roommate mediations. This is an opportunity for both roommates to communicate in a structured setting where the RA controls the conversation. Different mediation techniques are used, with the prevalent one being "I statements." This is where each person expresses concerns using "I statements," such as "I feel this way when you do this" or "I get irritated when you play your music so loud." Using these types of statements cuts down on the accusatory tones and the adversarial atmosphere that can potentially be created or may already be present.

Our staff is trained in mediation practices. The purpose of any mediation is to challenge the students to be able to communicate their concerns in a healthy manner. Not only does it teach communication, it forces the students to hold each other accountable for their behavior. It also teaches them that they cannot always run away from a problem or from people who are different from them.

CASE STUDY: ANDREW J. DIES

Living with a different person in close quarters, and even having issues with them, teaches many life lessons, which is an important component of living in the residence hall.

The biggest piece of advice is to be realistic, rather than idealistic, and to respect your fellow roommate. Understand that not everyone is like you. Not everyone is obsessive about the room being spotless. On the other hand, some people do care if you eat their food or use their computer. When doing preferences for the roommate agreement, and later in the year if problems crop up, being honest about your responses is key. Stating that you go to bed early just because Mom or Dad are standing right there while you fill out the form is not good if you plan to party every night. Be honest, be open, and be willing to compromise. All the preference questions in the world will not solve all issues that come up.

Communication is also vital. Talk about issues as they arise, rather than letting them pile up until you explode for no reason at all. Be willing to talk about things and find some happy compromise with the issue. If there is no compromise, be open to the idea of sacrificing some things for the sake of the roommate relationship.

A room change should be the last resort. Running away from the problem does not solve or teach anything. Working through the issues can allow both parties to grow from the experience. If all other avenues have been exhausted, then a room change will fix the problem.

CASE STUDY: MICHAELS

Assistant vice president and director of University Housing at a large public institution in the Northeast

Part of the housing-application process includes completing a questionnaire about life-style preferences. Are you an early riser or a night owl? Do you smoke? What are your feelings about sharing items, such as stereos, clothes, and computers? About one-half of the questionnaires we receive are based on honest responses. Roommates should openly discuss life-style preferences before moving in. Roommates have a unique relationship as they are witness to intimate facets of someone's life style, but we encourage them to engage. Talk to your roommates and keep the lines of communication open. When there is a problem, try to bring about change without going to an authority figure.

CASE STUDY: MICHAELS

Parents who are overly involved, (we call them "helicopter" or "hovering" parents), will go online, log on to their child's account, and complete the housing application. In one instance, the parents assumed their child was a nonsmoker, so they went into his account and indicated that on the roommate-preference form. Their son was, unbeknownst to them, a smoker. The problem with parents being involved in these cases is that they present an idealistic rather than realistic view of their child.

Another problem we run into with parents being overly involved is that they may look at the research their child has done on a roommate on Facebook or MySpace and find out, for example, that the child is gay or an atheist. In these cases, we may receive anywhere between ten and 20 calls over the summer from parents demanding that a new roommate be assigned.

Our entire staff is trained in conflict resolution. When there is a problem and the conflict cannot be resolved by the roommates, our staff sits down with them and forms an agreement. They encourage an open conversation on what is being agreed upon and how they will react and treat that agreement. Clear expectations are outlined, as well as consequences if everyone does not meet them. This generation tends to be more passive/aggressive. It is hard to get them to talk openly and honestly. Everyone may leave a meeting in agreement, but, the next day, someone will say they did not get what they wanted and vent to parents, friends, and anyone who will listen, while in a heightened emotional state. Our job is to help them ascertain who is responsible for the conflict. We want to treat students fairly. We want to base decisions on reality not on perceptions.

When we cannot get to an agreement that sticks, we ask roommates to list their expectations and what the outcome should be if they are not met. We cannot arbitrarily move one student and not the other, especially when neither has violated any policies. When there is a stalemate, we tell them they will both be moved and then they are more willing to work out the conflict, especially if there is no space to accommodate them. The last straw is offering them the option of being released from their contract without penalty.

Appendix E:
Off-Campus Housing Rental Inspection Checklist

SAMPLE RENTAL INSPECTION CHECKLIST (BASED ON 3 ROOMS)			
ITEM	ROOM	MOVE-IN CONDITION	MOVE-OUT CONDITION
Ceilings/walls			
Windows/doors			
Floors/tiles			
Ceilings/walls			
Windows/doors			
Floors/tiles			
Ceilings/walls			
Windows/doors			
Floors/tiles			
Water pressure			
Heater			
Hot water			
Leaks/drains/sink			
Toilet/shower			
Bugs			

SAMPLE RENTAL INSPECTION CHECKLIST (BASED ON 3 ROOMS)			
ITEM	ROOM	MOVE-IN CONDITION	MOVE-OUT CONDITION
Light fixtures			
Bathrooms Condition			
Kitchen			
Appliances			
Other items			

TO BE COMPLETED AT MOVE-IN ONLY

Tenant(s):_____   Date: _____

Landlord: _____   Date: _____

Witness: _____   Date: _____

TO BE COMPLETED AT MOVE-OUT ONLY

Tenant(s):_____   Date: _____

Landlord: _____   Date: _____

Witness: _____   Date: _____

Appendix F: Resources

General

Penn State University (Negotiating a Compromise): **www.psu. edu**

University of Central Florida (Preparing Students for Living with Roommates):

www.housing.ucf.edu/current/current.php.

Association of College and University Housing Officers-International:

www.acuho-i.org

www.collegeview.com (comprehensive site includes discussion forums, financial-aid information, college search and admissions information)

www.collegeconfidential.com (comprehensive site includes discussion forums, financial-aid information, college search and admissions information)

www.dormbuys.com (all kinds of items for your dorm room)

www.Amazon.com (search for books on college admissions, financial aid, and roommate problems)

Nifty Notes: *Roommate FYI Behavior Correction Note Pad*. Can be purchased online or at office supply stores.

Mental Health and Substance Abuse

Suicide Hot Line: 1-800-784-2433, open 24 hours a day, seven days a week

National Hopeline Network: 1-800-442-4673, **www.hopeline. com**

American Foundation for Suicide Prevention: **www.afsp.org**

Al-Anon/Alateen — Friends and Families of Alcoholics: **www. al-ateen.org**

National Mental Health Information Center: **www.mentalhealth. org**

National Institute of Mental Health: **www.nimh.org**

HealthyPlace.com: **www.healthyplace.com** (online depression resource and community)

Campus Blues: **www.campusblues.com**

National Association of Anorexia and Associated Disorders: **www.anad.org**

National Eating Disorders Association: **www.NationalEating-Disorders.org**

www.collegedrinkingprevention.gov

Poison Control Center: **1-800-222-1222**

Safety and Health

National Sexual Assault Hot Line: 1-800-656-HOPE

College Safety Guide: To download, visit **www.collegesafe.com**

Allergy and Asthma Network/Mothers of Asthmatics, Inc. (AAN/MA) **www.aanma.org**

Gay, Lesbian, Bisexual and Transgender

Gay & Lesbian Hot Line: 1-888-843-4564 or visit **www.glnh.org**

Parents, Families & Friends of Gays & Lesbians: **www.pflag.org**

National Coalition for Gay, Lesbian, Bisexual & Transgender Youth: **www.outproud.org**

Lambda Legal & Educational Defense Fund: **www.lambdalegal.net**

American Civil Liberties Union: **www.aclu.org**

Off-campus Housing

www.campus1housing.com (comprehensive site, searchable by college, for off-campus housing)

www.campusroommates.com (includes a comprehensive listing of ads that are specific to a college or university)

www.craigslist.com (free site to find and post cheap stuff, roommates, services)

www.roommates.com (searchable roommate database by state)

www.campusroommates.com (searchable database by state, college, city. Ads can be posted also)

Bibliography

You may find these books on conflict resolution, college roommates, and personality differences to be helpful:

Bernstein, M. and Y. Kaufmann, creators, *How to Survive Your Freshman Year*, Hundreds of Heads Books, LLC, Atlanta, GA, 2008.

Brinkman, R., and R. Kirschner, *Dealing With People You Can't Stand*, McGraw-Hill, Inc., New York, NY, 2002.

Cohen, H., *The Naked Roommate*, Sourcebooks, Inc., Naperville, IL, 2005.

Deutsch, M., P. Coleman, and E. Marcus, eds. *The Handbook of Conflict Resolution*, Jossey-Bass, San Francisco, CA, 2006.

Harrison, Jr., H., *1001 Things Every College Student Needs to Know*, Thomas Nelson, Nashville, TN, 2008.

Janson, J., *The Real Freshman Handbook: A Totally Honest Guide to Life on Campus*, Houghton Mifflin Company, New York, NY, 2002.

Podlasiak, M., *Rules for Roommates*, Writers Club Press, New York, NY, 2000.

Scott, G. Graham, *A Survival Guide for Working with Humans*, AMACON, New York, NY, 2004.

Scott, G. Graham, *Disagreements, Disputes, and All-Out War*, AMACON, New York, NY, 2008.

"When Girls Will Be Boys," *New York Times Magazine*, March 2008, pp. 32-37.

Coburn Levin, K. and Treeger, M. Lawrence, *Letting Go: A Parents' Guide to Understanding the College Years, Fourth Edition*, HarperCollins, New York, NY, 2003.

Malone, M., *The Everything College Survival Book: From Social Life To Study Skills — All You Need To Fit Right In (Everything: School and Careers)*, Adams Media, Avon, MA, 1997, 2005.

Johnston, J. and Shanley, M., *Survival Secrets of College Students*, Barron's Educational Series, Inc., Hauppauge, NY, 2007.

Piven, J., Borgenicht, D., Worick, J. and Brown, B., *Worst-Case Scenario Survival Handbook: College*, Chronicle Books, LLC, San Francisco, CA, 2004.

Farrar, R. and Worthington, J., *The Ultimate College Survival Guide, Fourth Edition (Ultimate College Survival Guide)*, Peterson's Educational Center, **www.petersons.com**.

Antinozzi. G. and Axelrod, A., *The Complete Idiot's Guide to Campus Safety*, Alpha Books, Published by the Penguin Group, New York, NY, 2008.

Dobkin, R. and Sippy, S., *The College Woman's Handbook,* Workman Publishing Company, Inc., New York, NY, 1995.

Leinwand, D., *College drug use, binge drinking rise*, USA TODAY, The Associated Press, 2007.

Lang, S., *Self-injury is prevalent among college students, but few seek medical help, study by Cornell and Princeton researchers finds*, Cornell University, Chronicle Online, June 5, 2006, **www.news.cornell.edu**.

Hitti, M., *College Students May Hide Self-Harm*, WebMD Medical News, June 6, 2006, **www.webmd.com**.

About the Author

Linda Fiore has worked in education for more than 20 years. In addition to her research and writing on education, she was executive director of a Philadelphia-based nonprofit arts-education organization, taught music in public and private schools, and is the Director of College Relations and External Affairs for the Boyer College of Music and Dance at Temple University. She is also a freelance writer and has published extensively on arts education, public arts and cultural policy, nonprofit leadership, and local history. She is editor of several higher-education publications, and serves on boards and panels of Philadelphia cultural organizations and academic institutions.

She studied at the Boston Conservatory of Music and holds a B.A. in music from the University of Maryland, a M.MusicEd from the University of Portland, and an M.S. in Arts Administration from Drexel University.

Researching this book and interviewing past and current college roommates has brought back fond, and not-so-fond, memories of the author's own roommate experience more than 30 years ago in a cramped dorm off the Fenway in Boston.

Index

OFF TO COLLEGE: NOW WHAT? A PRACTICAL GUIDE TO SURVIVING AND SUCCEEDING YOUR FIRST YEAR OF COLLEGE

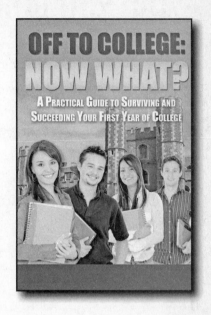

Attending college can be an exciting and frightening experience. You will be on your own for the first time, meeting new friends and learning new ideas. The experience can become a little intimidating, but it does not have to.

Off to College: Now What? gives you insight on the college experience. You will learn about the new situations you will be presented with while in college. The author leaves no stone unturned, teaching you about classes, dorms, greek life, sex, and dating. You will also learn how to maintain a strict, organized schedule, balance your free time, and study properly.

This book helps prepare you for any conflicts that might arise once you are at college. It will help you transition seamlessly from high school into college.

ISBN-10: 1-60138-314-2 • ISBN-13: 978-1-60138-314-3
288 Pages • Item # CGB-02 • $24.95

DID YOU BORROW THIS COPY?

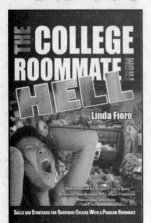

Have you been borrowing a copy of *The College Roommate from Hell: Skills and Strategies for Surviving College With a Problem Roommate* from a friend, colleague, or library? Wouldn't you like your own copy for quick and easy reference? To order, photocopy the form below and send to:

Atlantic Publishing Company

1405 SW 6th Ave • Ocala, FL 34471-0640